ROMMEL
IN NORTH AFRICA

D. A. Lande

MBI Publishing Company

Onward he rolls triumphant,
Naming countries, in his track . . .
On he rushes, unrelenting,
Leaving the turrets tipped with flame . . .

—from "Mahomets Gesang" (A Song to Mahomet)
by Johann Wolfgang von Goethe (1749–1832)

First published in 1999 by MBI Publishing Company, 729 Prospect Avenue, PO Box 1, Osceola, WI 54020-0001 USA

© D. A. Lande, 1999

The information in this book is true and complete to the best of our knowledge. All recommendations are made without any guarantee on the part of the author or Publisher, who also disclaim any liability incurred in connection with the use of this data or specific details.

We recognize that some words, model names and designations, for example, mentioned herein are the property of the trademark holder. We use them for identification purposes only. This is not an official publication.

MBI Publishing Company books are also available at discounts in bulk quantity for industrial or sales-promotional use. For details write to Special Sales Manager at Motorbooks International Wholesalers & Distributors, 729 Prospect Avenue, Osceola, WI 54020-0001 USA.

Library of Congress Cataloging-in-Publication Data

Lande, D. A.,
    Rommel in North Africa / D. A. Lande.
        p.   cm.
    Includes index.
    ISBN 0-7603-0591-9 (pbk. : alk. paper)
    1. Africa, North—History. Military. [1. World War. 1939–1945—Campaigns—Africa, North. 2. Rommel, Erwin, 1891–1944.]
    I. Title.
D766.82.L36   1999   98-54882
940.54'23—dc21

On the front cover: Standing in his command car, Rommel is the master of all he surveys . . . at least for the time being. The German commander's constant presence on the front lines was an inspiration to his men and the key to his hands-on style of leadership. The Desert Fox always wanted to see the action and direct it personally, changing tactics as the battle ebbed and flowed. *National Archives*

On the back cover: (Top) Tanks, half-tracks, trucks, and artillery, probably of the 90th Panzer Division, press on to the coastal town of Bardia. Terrain is such that vehicles can drive many abreast on firm ground. The approach to Bardia was actually a ruse; just as the British became convinced the column had its sites set on Bardia (where the British were on full alert for a division-strength assault), Rommel suddenly turned his column left and bore down on Tobruk. That night, as Rommel directed his units into position in the old familiar territory just south of Tobruk (where they had tried before to seize it and failed), they found undisturbed supply dumps just where they'd left them the previous April, with even more artillery shells with which to pound Tobruk. *Rommelarchiv*

(Bottom) After defeat in North Africa, Rommel returned to Germany. Hitler summoned him to his headquarters soon after the Axis surrender at Tunis in May 1943. Rommel attempted to convince him that the only recourse for Germany was to seek "peace with conditions." Hitler disregarded the voice of reason and declared, "Remember, nobody will make peace with me!" *National Archives*

Excerpts from *The Rommel Papers*, copyright 1953 by B. H. Liddell-Hart and renewed 1981 by Lady Kathleen Liddell-Hart, Fritz Bayerlein-Dittmar, and Manfred Rommel, reprinted by permission of Harcourt Brace & Company.

Edited by Christopher Batio
Designed by Rebecca Allen

Printed in the United States of America.

CONTENTS

ACKNOWLEDGMENTS

Rommel wrote extensively of his World War II experience in North Africa. His writings were posthumously published as *Krieg ohne Hass*, much of which was translated and published as *The Rommel Papers*, edited by B. H. Liddell Hart. My thanks to the publisher of *The Rommel Papers*, Harcourt, Brace and Company, for permission to quote from Rommel's words. All epigraphs and other individual Rommel quotations come from *The Rommel Papers*, unless otherwise noted.

A succession of authors, starting with Desmond Young, have kept alive the memory of Erwin Rommel through the decades since World War II. Their studies of Rommel (published in Great Britain, Germany, and America), and Rommel's own writings, provided a basis for this book.

I have also drawn from written and photographic material found in Germany at the Bundesarchiv in Koblenz, the Rommelarchiv in Herrlingen, and the Bundesarchiv-Militararchiv in Freiburg. Special thanks to the curators of Rommelarchiv for their warm welcome and the privilege of trust granted to this foreign author. Also thanks to Ms. Caspers and other staff of Bundesarchiv for their patient help in identifying photographs and documents.

Much material also was found at the National Archives in College Park, Maryland. My thanks for assistance in extensive photo searches there. Thanks also to the Dwight D. Eisenhower Library in Abilene, Kansas.

Most of all, special thanks to individuals who contributed generously to the project: Isabelle Engels, for helping me find my way through Germany and its archives. Angelika Haas, for her insights and translations. Albert and Ilse Haas for incredible generosity and kindness in Germany. And Dave Kaphingst, for his photo reproduction expertise.

INTRODUCTION

Germany's most famous and respected military leader of World War II was Field Marshal Erwin Rommel. He became a world figure when his dramatic victories stunned British forces in the Western Desert of North Africa during 1941 and 1942.

Rommel's wartime exploits actually began with infantry action in World War I, when he won the *Pour le Mérité*, Imperial Germany's highest decoration for valor. His career concluded with his command of the Atlantic Wall defenses late in World War II. However, this book's central focus is the period for which Rommel is known best—his 25-month campaign in North Africa. The time frame is February 1941, when Rommel first arrived in Tripoli, through March 1943, when he relinquished command and departed Africa, never to return.

Rommel's desert war was like a series of roller coaster ups and downs. It can be described in four oscillating phases: Victory, then retreat, followed by victory, then defeat. This book's structure details that series of ups and downs. The first two chapters set the stage, with an overview of Rommel's life and the creation of the Afrika Korps. The following chapters and the greater portion of the book cover the stunning first triumphs, when Rommel took all of Cyrenaica; the

hard fall of 1941, when he extended his forces beyond supply capability; the lightning turnaround, when he retook lost ground and more; and finally, the Armageddon that ended the Axis campaign in Africa.

This book is intended to be broad in scope, with photos in equal proportion to text. The size and structure do not provide the means to delve into the great complexities of Rommel's desert victories or all aspects of Rommel as a man; instead, it offers a visual and verbal overview of those eventful two years in his life. If your interest in Rommel is piqued and you wish to learn more, many books and other sources concentrate on specific facets of the desert campaign and Rommel's entire career as a military leader. Whole volumes are devoted to capturing every known detail of the sieges at El Alamein, Tobruk, the "Cauldron," and Kasserine Pass, along with other individual campaigns and Rommel's succession of commands elsewhere.

History has been kind to some military leaders and cruel to others. It has treated Rommel very favorably. He is one of the few German leaders of World

Rommel's woolen continental service cap, with peaked crown and gold braid. Mounted on the visor are British Perspex goggles, the ones Rommel wore in the desert. These are on display, along with many other artifacts, at the Rommelarchiv in Herrlingen, Germany. *Author's collection*

5

War II who is heralded almost universally for his leadership qualities and tactical genius.

Rommel emerged from the annals of that horrible war and the atrocities of Hitler somehow untainted by the heinous nature of Nazism. He is remembered as fighting "clean," for his humane treatment of prisoners, and for his great patriotism for Germany. These are certainly honorable—and true depictions, as documented repeatedly in both Allied and Axis accounts.

Rommel's story has a way of arousing the tendency in many of us to "pull for the underdog," which he

Erwin Rommel poses with the field marshal's baton presented to him by Hitler. He was promoted to field marshal in June 1942, just after the capture of Tobruk. The rank of field marshal is the equivalent of a five-star general in the American rank structure. *Rommelarchiv*

almost always was. By using bold strategies, brilliant deception, swift maneuver, and uncanny anticipation of the enemy's moves, he routinely won battles despite facing numerically superior opponents. In the process, he shattered the confidence of numerous Allied commanders.

Nonetheless, he did fight on the side of Nazism, even though he declined to join the Nazi party. He fought for Germany, but not for the Nazi cause. In this way, he can be likened to another great commander, U.S. Civil War General Robert E. Lee, who fought for his beloved Virginia but did not believe in the Confederate cause of slavery. Rommel *is* known to have been devoted to Nazi leader Adolf Hitler. His death by Hitler's command seems to only add to Rommel's image of heroism and anti-Nazism. However, his death by Hitler's order doesn't excuse him for this misguided devotion, which shaped so much of his career.

What helps further separate him from the Nazis is a unique scenario: In Africa, Rommel developed and worked within a *Wehrgemeinschaft*—a military unit functioning by virtue of its own internal dynamics, as opposed to imposed discipline and direction. In this environment, Rommel's troops didn't question why they fought. In this way, they borrowed on the age-old philosophy of the French Foreign Legion, whose men find their advantage in "fighting for the Legion, not for an idea."

Isolation in the desert benefited Rommel in a number of ways. The distance from Berlin allowed him to fight the desert campaign his own way, largely unimpeded by Hitler's influence and the interference of others in the German High Command. (He wasn't immune from this kind of interference, but compared to his counterparts on the Continent, he operated very freely.)

Plus, Rommel was a "simple soldier," who fulfilled the conventional role of carrying out policy but not making it. Like nearly all Wehrmacht officers of the time, Rommel avoided politics and affiliation with political parties, including the Nazi Party. His sole interest was in developing his leadership ability and perfecting the art of warfare. There were no politics to be played in the desert anyway. It was the purest form of all-out war with no intricate or hidden agendas . . . and few innocent civilians to get in the way. In the desert, there is virtually nothing to hurt except your enemy.

So, just as Rommel's focus remained on the battles of the desert (and not the larger picture of the politics that sent him there), this book remains focused on Rommel as a leader and the desert battles that earned him a place in history. The interpretations presented here are solely those of your author, not of the publisher.

Chapter One

THE MYSTERIOUS DESERT FOX

Cunning. Chivalrous. Victorious. These were common words used to describe Erwin Rommel in his lifetime and since his death. Such descriptions appeared not only in German propaganda of the day, but in the world press as well. For any military leader to be recognized this way, by both friend and foe, was astonishing. But then, Rommel himself was astonishing.

He was a paradox. As a military leader, he was bold in strategy, ferocious in attack, relentless in pursuit, and obsessed with attaining his objective. Yet even under the maniacal leadership of Adolf Hitler, Rommel maintained uncommon human decency and chivalry in wartime. He became known for his humane treatment of Allied prisoners in North Africa, where he ordered rations of food and water and medical treatment for the captured men equal to that given to his own troops. This equal treatment was also extended to a Jewish brigade captured near Bir Hacheim.

> "The commander's place is not back with his staff but up with the troops. . . . In moments of panic, fatigue or disorganization, or when something out of the ordinary has to be demanded from them, the personal example of the commander works wonders, especially if he has had the wit to create some sort of legend round himself."
>
> —Erwin Rommel

Rommel was the consummate professional soldier. It set him apart, and gave the Allies a personage to visualize and refer to, instead of talking vaguely about the faceless conquering machine of Nazi Germany.

Before early 1941, British newspapers had not yet picked up on his name. At that time, reporters sometimes still referred to German forces collectively and contemptuously as "the Hun" or "Boches," phrases left over from World War I. The new, highly mechanized German army remained an enigma—a rampaging behemoth made of steel carried along on tank tracks.

But with a series of stunning victories in 1941, the name Rommel emerged from the desert sands to become synonymous with the adjectives that lead off this page. Phantom-like powers were attributed to him, because he always seemed to appear in places least expected. Always commanding forces inferior in numbers and firepower. Always seeming to anticipate his adversaries' next move. Always somehow escaping injury or worse from shells and bombs exploding around him . . . and winning victory after victory.

Headlines changed overnight from the vague, impersonal news of "2,000 British Prisoners Taken" and "Greater Enemy Activity in Libya" to the very personal "Rommel's Panzer Division Hitting Back" and "Rommel's New Thrust." *The Times* of London and other newspapers around the world would feature his name innumerable times during the years to come.

At first, the press outside Germany unwittingly paid him this accolade of recognition. Later, they deliberately played up his name because he, as an individual, became news. Few other Wehrmacht commanders were even recognized by name, let alone in such a prominent way.

The world's leaders, most notably British Prime Minister Winston Churchill, referred to Rommel by name over and over again. In mid-August 1942, an impassioned Churchill bellowed to Parliament: "Rommel, Rommel, Rommel, Rommel! What else matters but beating him?" Churchill also referred to him as "a master of war" and chastised his own Middle East commander by saying "Rommel has torn the new-won laurels from Wavell's brow and thrown them in the sand." Amazingly, through his enemy's speeches, Rommel's fame spread and his reputation grew to legendary proportions the world over.

Rommel's appearance became familiar as well. A distinct image was burned into the minds of friend and foe: The trademark visor cap with goggles resting over the gold braid. Intense blue-gray eyes burning like coals in the visor's shadow. High cheek bones. A firm, determined, defiant jaw. Binoculars hanging from his neck. He was not tall in stature, but what he lacked in height he made up for in self-confidence and an extraordinarily supreme air of command.

Germany's propaganda cameras made Rommel one of World War II's most photographed soldiers.

Usually, the photographs captured him in action. Although some photos seem staged in overdramatic poses for propaganda purposes, he *was* in action on the front lines constantly among his troops, as illustrated in the quotation that leads off this chapter.

Rommel understood the art of propaganda and availed himself to it for the psychological value it had on his troops and his adversaries. The German public and military knew of him even before the North African victories. He had authored a best-selling book in 1937 titled *Infanterie Greift an (Infantry Attacks)* that recorded, in spirited fashion, effective infantry tactics drawn from his battlefield experience in World War I. His military genius and leadership style is there for the reader to see. In the blitzkrieg through the Ardennes and northern France in 1940, he had commanded the 7th Panzer Division, the first to fight its way to the English Channel (for which he was awarded the Knight's Cross). Dr. Joseph Goebbels' propaganda writers glorified Rommel, and he let them build this image.

The blitzkrieg put Rommel's name on the lips of people throughout his homeland, more than even celebrities of the day. But the same blitzkrieg victory that made his name widely known in Germany also drew resentment from many in the Wehrmacht's officer ranks. Much of this feeling was born of petty professional jealousy, but some criticism was legitimate. Rommel's rapid advance past the Meuse River and Maginot Line was at the expense of other German divisions—made possible by diverting supplies to his own troops from other commands. The resulting Knight's Cross and public fame further fanned the flame of ire in the older, established generals, who viewed Rommel as a young and aggressive upstart. He would always remain an outsider to the German general staff.

Rommel was one of those people prone to be regarded in extremes, resented by some and revered by

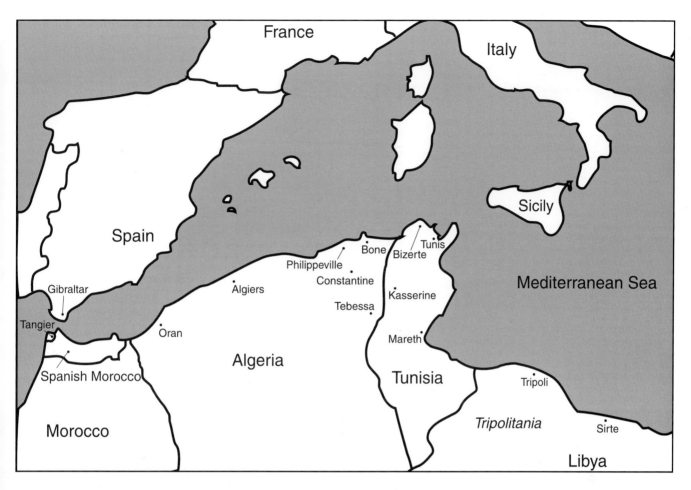

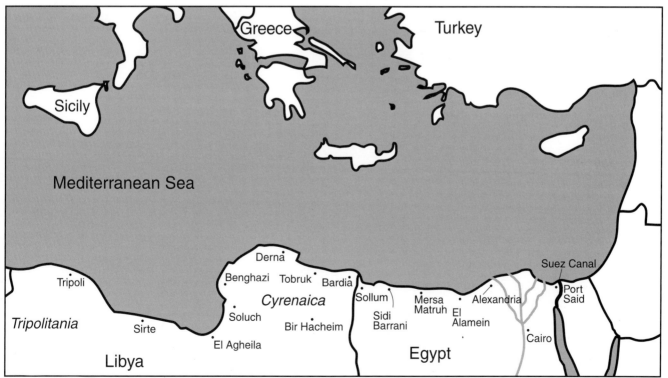

Watchful and ready to exploit enemy weaknesses, Rommel was always present on the front lines of battle, rather than in the safety of rear headquarters. Some soldiers said, "Where Rommel is, so is the battle." Observing firsthand, he evaluated and reevaluated his battle plan, often changing tank and troop movements on a moment's notice. He relied on flexibility and mobility—uniquely possible with armored forces in the desert—to outfox his enemy. Common sense methods like these inspired a belief that Rommel had a "sixth sense" on the battlefield—a mysterious perception that enabled him to know enemy moves in advance. *National Archives*

others. Inside his own army, he exasperated his peers with sudden changes of orders and a sometimes undiplomatic manner. But he was revered by the combat troops. He talked with them. They saw him eating, sleeping and risking his life as they did. So they also witnessed his moodiness, his impatience, his forceful speech, his explosive temper, his unwillingness to admit mistakes, his merciless scrutiny of tactical details, his inspired but erratic decisions. His demands were extremely high, but each man knew that what was demanded was within his capability. Rommel gave no order that he himself would not have been willing to carry out. He was unrelenting, yet completely unassuming. He was quick with praise for a job well done. The men saw a softness in his eyes, sensed his devotion to them and, despite a hardened exterior, suspected a heart as vast as the desert itself. They knew his resolve, his will to prevail, his penchant for victory. Consequently, the performance he inspired in them was beyond reasonable expectation.

He had a cool, logical mind, developed through three decades as a line officer. His clear and precise writing reflects that. Yet his more brilliant command decisions seem based on instinct rather than intellect.

Winston Churchill, highly vocal and pointed in commentaries about the African Theater, frequently talked about Rommel as an individual. While he publicly chastised his own African commanders, Churchill openly praised Rommel: "We have a very daring and skillful opponent against us, and, may I say, across the havoc of war, a great general." *National Archives*

British troops also came to fear and respect him. Their awe caused such a stir that General C. J. Auchinleck, Rommel's counterpart in the British command, issued this directive to his officer staff: "There exists a real danger that our friend Rommel is becoming a kind of magician or bogey-man to our troops, who are talking far too much about him. Even if he were a superman, it would still be highly undesirable that our men should credit him with supernatural powers."

This attribution of "supernatural powers" resulted from talk among troops that Rommel had a sixth sense—a heightened sensitivity for the dynamics of the battlefield. Troops of the Afrika Korps came to

Authored by Rommel in 1937, *Infanterie Greift an (Infantry Attacks)* encapsulates his combat experience in World War I. At the time he wrote it, Rommel was an *oberstleutnant* (lieutenant colonel) and instructor at the Infantry School in Potsdam. The book project began when Rommel organized his lecture notes from his infantry tactics course into chapter form and edited them in present tense. Then he submitted it to a local publisher. Probably the best infantry tactics book of its time, the book sold so well that it went into many subsequent editions. Ironically, in 1944, the year of Rommel's death, the book was translated and published in English. Note the name at the top. How "Von" found its way into Rommel's name on the English edition is unknown. Perhaps the publisher wanted to lend nobility to the author, even though Rommel's family was not among the privileged class. The highest echelons of the aristocratic German *Wehrmacht* had been dominated for generations by blue-blooded "vons" such as von Ravenstein, von Rundstedt, von Brauchitsch, and von Arnim. The original cover, published in German, read "Oberstleutnant Rommel" and the title, nothing more. *Author's collection*

General Rommel is greeted by Nazi Propaganda Minister Joseph Goebbels in Berlin on March 10, 1942. Goebbels was one of the few men in the Nazi hierarchy whom Rommel respected. At this time, Rommel had just returned from Africa and the second Cyrenaica offensive. Three months later, he would stun the Allies by taking Tobruk. On his next trip to Berlin, he would be a field marshal. *Bundesarchiv*

German propaganda cameras roll as a Panzer IV crew reenacts scenes from the blitzkrieg in France. Rommel's panzer division is featured in the film for reaching the French coast first. The film includes plenty of recognition for Rommel as leader. *National Archives*

label it *Fingerspitzengefühl*, which translates into "intuition in the fingertips."

Out of this mystique, the legend of Rommel grew during World War II. He became a military meteor, experiencing a rocket-like rise to victory and fame, followed by an equally accelerated descent and burn-up. He went from lieutenant colonel to field marshal in four years. Then, just two years later, he would be murdered by his own countrymen.

It was through his desert victories that he became more of a "bogey-man" than a flesh-and-blood human being. Much about him was unknown, partly because he didn't have a colorful background outside of the war and his military service. Mystique and rumors rose up to fill the void around him. Fueled by Nazi propaganda, talk circulated through the British ranks of a more dramatic and unsavory past for Rommel. "He was one of the first Nazi stormtroopers," some Tommies said over morning tea. Other rumors exaggerated his humble beginnings saying he was "the son of a laborer" and an enlisted man who had risen through the ranks in World War I. There was also talk that he had been a policeman in the interwar years. A prevailing thought, which continued even after the war, was that he was an original Nazi party member along with Martin Bormann, Ernst Rohm, Rudolf Hess, and Hermann Goering. It was said he

Young for his rank, Rommel was a born leader. In four short years he went from lieutenant colonel, through full colonel and the four German ranks of general, and on to field marshal. When he visited the fighting front, troops hung on his every word and lionized him. Those feelings were not typically shared by subordinate staff officers, like those shown here, who felt he was explosive in mood and unreasonable in expectations. Other generals often viewed him as an aggressive and under-educated upstart. *National Archives*

headed up bullying gangs of Hitler's brown-shirted S.A. on the streets of Germany. None of this was accurate.

The "real" Rommel was explainable and very human. He assumed legendary proportions in an age when men and women had a greater readiness to accept heroes and villains without question, and allow mere mortals to grow larger than life.

Erwin Johannes Eugen Rommel was born at noon on November 15, 1891, in Heidenheim, near Ulm, in the southern province of Germany called Wurttemberg. He was the son and grandson of schoolmasters. Young Erwin was a quiet, athletic boy, skilled in downhill skiing, hiking and cycling. In an application to Royal Officer Cadet School in Danzig, his father described him simply as "Thrifty, reliable and a good gymnast."

Germany's highest decoration for valor: the *Pour le Mérité*, also known as the Blue Max. Rommel won the award for an almost unbelievable tactical feat in October 1917. As a young officer with five years of service and in command of only a few hundred German troops, he captured 8,000 enemy soldiers. Ironically, they were 8,000 *Italian* soldiers, captured in the snowy Isonzo sector of northern Italy (ironic considering he would command many Italian divisions in the next war). The decoration was also awarded to another young German whose martial feats during World War I became legendary—Manfred von Richthofen, the Red Baron. *Rommelarchiv*

In Robert Leckie's epic saga of World War II titled *Delivered from Evil*, Erwin's only sister described him as " . . . a very gentle and docile child. Small for his age, he had a white skin and hair so pale that we called him the 'white Teddy bear.' He spoke very slowly and only after reflecting for a long time. He was very good tempered and amiable and not afraid of anyone."

His family did not have a military tradition, unlike many in the aristocratic Wehrmacht who came from long successive lines of military officers. Nor did he have any advantages accorded the privileged classes. But he was accepted as an officer cadet and, although he was not a standout among his schoolmates, he was eventually commissioned a second lieutenant in the 126th Wurttemberg Infantry Regiment in 1912. This was timely, since World War I broke out two years later and Rommel quickly gained the opportunity to show his battle prowess. In peacetime, Rommel might have seemed like a common, even dull, soldier, whose highest aspirations were to reach the rank of major, retire on a meager pension, never having emerged from obscurity. But the heat of battle fired his imagination and drew out his strategic genius. This made 1914 through 1917 and 1940 through 1943 the brief but extremely eventful years upon which his entire life and legend would be built.

Rommel was a tremendous risk-taker on the battlefield, oftentimes gambling on his instincts and usually winning. He struggled hard to rise above the rest and was proud of his achievements.

During World War I, when he was in his early to mid-20s, Rommel won his country's highest decoration for valor, the *Pour le Mérité*. The decoration was usually reserved for senior officers, but when awarded to junior officers, the *Pour le Mérité* was the equivalent to the U.S. Medal of Honor and Britain's Victoria Cross. The award came for an extraordinary victory in October 1917, when Rommel, as a junior officer commanding only a few hundred troops in the snowy Isonzo sector of northern Italy, captured 8,000 Italian soldiers, said to be a record for any German officer during the war. He also won the Iron Cross, second class, in 1914 and Iron Cross, first class, in 1915.

He married during the war while on leave from the Rumanian front in November 1916. His wife was Lucie Maria Mollin, to whom he would remain devoted for his entire life. His almost daily letters to her during World War II always began with the salutation "Dear Lu." They are rarely intimate (nor were her letters to him), but they reveal some gut feelings and other emotions not explicit in his notes about the African campaign. Lucie gave birth to their only child, a son named Manfred, in 1928.

After Rommel's stunning victory in the first Cyrenaican campaign, talk among the British Tommies began to proliferate. Their stories became more elaborate and dramatic, until Rommel had became a "bogey-man," according to British General Sir Claude Auchinleck. With each successive Rommel victory, the legend grew. *National Archives*

Newly commissioned in the Wurttemberg 124th Infantry Regiment, Rommel is fresh out of the Royal Officers Cadet School at Danzig, where he had been a serious, albeit average, student. At the time, his instructors might have scoffed had they been told about the future that lay before him. *Rommelarchiv*

During the years following World War I, Rommel remained a line officer. Competence and hard work elevated him through the hierarchy of the Wehrmacht. His regimental commander wrote of him in 1934: "Head and shoulders above the average battalion commander in every respect."

As the Nazi Party rose to power during the tumultuous 1930s, Rommel declined to join. In fact, he deliberately sidestepped politics and affiliation with parties, and abhorred the brutal methods of the brown-shirted thugs of the S.A. He was simply a professional army officer—a "common soldier"—focused on the military's traditional role of carrying out the nation's policies, rather than making them.

By most accounts, Rommel's path did not cross Hitler's until September 1934. At the time, Rommel was 43-year-old lieutenant colonel serving at Goslar in the Harz Mountains, where he had commanded a mountain *jaeger* (riflemen) battalion since the previous October. Hitler came to the area to meet with a farmers' delegation and (in the usual Nazi display of pomp) to parade through the streets with marching bands and armed troops. Hitler inspected elements of Rommel's battalion, which were to serve as honor guard in the parade. It's believed that was the first face-to-face salute, and possibly handshake, exchanged between the two.

"Dear Lu,"

the recipient of many letters that give insights into her husband's character. Lucie Maria Mollin became Rommel's wife, confidante, friend, and one true love of his life. During World War I, he met and married Lucie, who gave birth to their only child, Manfred, in 1928. Here she poses in a late 1930s photo (while Manfred clowns in the background using a camera lens cap as a monocle behind his mother). Rommelarchiv

Rommel poses with his wife, Lucie, and his son, Manfred, who is about 11 or 12 here. Several years later, Manfred would learn many of his famous father's inner thoughts during the last weeks of his life, after the wounded field marshal had returned to the family home in Herrlingen. *National Archives*

In **1937,** *Rommel became the War Ministry's liaison to Hitler Youth. Although the assignment didn't last long because of immediate conflicts with Hitler Youth leader Baldur von Schirach, Rommel once noted that he found "real joy working with the lads."* Author's collection

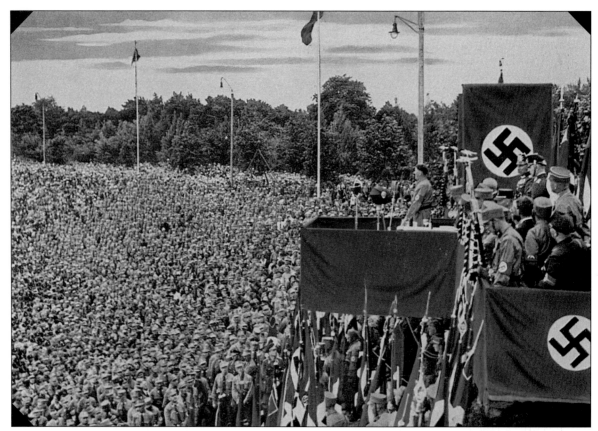

A Nazi Party rally *in Dortmund, 1933. Erwin Rommel was not present in the sea of faces. He was not an active member of any political party and abhorred the brown-shirted thugs of Ernst Rohm's Sturmabteilung, the SA, which bullied a path for the Nazi Party's rise to power.* Author's collection

Ernst Rohm (second from right) and Heinrich Himmler (far right) were two of the original henchmen of the Nazi Party. Here they are seen with Hitler in Leipzig during an SA rally in 1933. *Author's collection*

Soon after, when Rommel brought his battalion to form up for the parade, he found that a line of SS troops in their striking black uniforms were to be posted at the head of his battalion as the lead guard for *Der Fuhrer*. Rommel was extremely offended by this, because it suggested that his mountain commandos were not capable of protecting their distinguished visitor. He immediately threatened to march them home if the SS weren't removed.

This incident illuminates something of Rommel's character. Asserting himself in this way was an extraordinarily bold stroke in 1930's Germany. Himmler and Goebbels were said to be present and the SS was given wide latitude by even the highest ranking officers in the Wehrmacht. In the end, the order of the SS was rescinded, and Rommel's unit marched alone with Hitler.

Rommel eventually was promoted to full colonel and personally selected by Hitler himself to be commander of the unit charged with protecting him during the march into Czechoslovakia's Sudetenland in October 1938. The *Fuhrerbegleitbattailon* was an elite battalion whose sole responsibility was *Der Fuhrer's* personal safety.

It was in this post that Rommel began to gain Hitler's attention. Hitler no doubt noticed the *Pour le Mérité* and became aware of *Infanterie Greift an*. Given

Rommel's mountain battalion served as honor guard for Hitler in a parade like this in September 1938. This passing introduction led to Rommel's eventual appointment as commander of the *Fuhrerbegleitbattailon*, the battalion responsible for Der Fuhrer's personal safety. The appointment marked the beginning of a budding relationship between the two. *Author's collection*

Hitler converses with his favorite general. Explaining why Rommel was given command in Africa, *Der Fuhrer* simply stated, "I picked him because he knows how to inspire his troops." *National Archives*

Hitler's racist ideals, he was probably also impressed with Rommel's blue-eyed and blond Nordic appearance.

Rommel enjoyed the recognition of *Der Fuhrer* and the favor that came with it, like the preference in getting the command positions he so badly wanted. Rommel, in turn, was enamored with some of Hitler's personal characteristics, like his intensity and incredible discernment of other men's thoughts. But most of all, Rommel admired Hitler for unifying the German people and rearming the nation. The intensely patriotic Rommel's one true devotion was to Germany as a nation, so he pledged a soldier's allegiance to the leader of the Reich.

This led to his appointment as a panzer division commander in the blitzkrieg of 1940, when then-General Major Rommel would command the first of the German divisions to reach the coast of France. It was there he would begin World War II, and there he would end it, as commander of Army Group B, defending the shores of France, Belgium, and Holland against the anticipated Allied invasion. But what happened in between—the African campaign—is what secured him a place in history, where he will be forever known as The Desert Fox.

The first German division commander to reach the French coast, Rommel stands victorious among a group of vanquished British officers. An entire British division surrendered and its commander, Major General Victor Fortune (third from right), was among the first in a succession of Allied commanders to be humbled by Rommel in World War II. *National Archives*

Rommel looks on as a members of his staff communicate with French General Ihler, commander of the IX Corps at Saint-Valery on the English Channel. In German newsreels and media, Rommel was heralded throughout his homeland as the first to reach the Channel. *National Archives*

Rommel walks with the heavyweights of the Nazi regime. Beside him is Adolf Hitler and in the second rank is Hitler's secretary Martin Bormann and Field Marshal Wilhelm Keitel. As a German patriot, Rommel admired Hitler for uniting the nation, as well as his support of the army and decisive leadership at the outset of World War II. *Bundesarchiv*

Chapter Two

POISED TO STRIKE

Rommel's arrival in North Africa came just days after the Battle of Beda Fomm, where the British Western Desert Force had stamped an exclamation point on the overwhelming victory they had wrought over the humiliated Italian Army.

Rommel was dispatched to Africa with strictly a defensive mission: To prevent the British from completely annihilating the Italian Army that had once occupied much of North Africa. Rommel chafed under the binds of a defensive role, but accepted the assignment.

North Africa was important during World War II because of its strategic location. It was the key to control of the Suez Canal. More importantly, it had value as a stepping stone to the Persian Gulf nations. If control of North Africa and the Eastern Mediterranean region could be wrested from the British, a door would be opened to continue east and seize vital oil resources in Persia (Iran) and Iraq. And once across the Syrian

> *" . . . I reported to the Fuhrer, who gave me a detailed account of the situation in Africa and informed me that I had been recommended to him as the man who would most quickly adapt himself to the altogether different conditions of the African theater."*
>
> —Erwin Rommel

desert and through Persia, the Germans would find a vulnerable flank for an attack through the Caucasus into Russia. Controlling the North African coast would also give the Axis a way to threaten British bases on Malta and Cyprus, as well as further isolating the Empire's holdings in southern and eastern Africa.

North Africa presented a unique environment for warfare, and Rommel's victories there can be traced largely to his understanding of one simple principle—desert warfare is like battle at sea, and there is no point in occupying vast stretches of territory. Did it matter who occupied the trackless expanse of undulating waves in the ocean, or undulating dunes in the sand? It did not. Fixed points on the seascape or desert landscape have no value of their own, and there is no reason to defend a barren geographic point. The only geographic features in North Africa that had "value" were seaports and escarpment passes.

Rommel meets with Italian officers, including General Italo Gariboldi (left) in Tripoli. From the very start, Rommel's relationship with the Italian high command was rocky. At first, the Italians had refused Germany's help in North Africa. When they finally accepted it, they found themselves dealing with a strong-willed German general who was gifted as a soldier, but not as a diplomat. *National Archives*

What *did* matter was who could eliminate the enemy force while preserving his own. Rommel grasped this from the very beginning. Neither the British or the Italians, with their long-bred colonial mentality, understood these facts, until Rommel taught them.

The Beleaguered Italians

Benito Mussolini had been leader of the Italian Fascist state since 1922. In that time he had tripled his military forces in long-occupied Tripolitania, the western province of Libya. His grandiose dreams of reviving the Roman glory included expanding eastward in Africa.

Italian feeling toward its colonies was complex and deep rooted. Portions of North Africa were long-held Italian possessions, a playground where rich Italians owned beautiful villas along the coast. But the colonies were much more than that. They were a vestige of the Roman Empire, conquered by the once-great legions of Caesar, which had dominated ancient civilization and annexed much of the known world as its own. Mussolini saw himself as the new Roman emperor, who would restore his nation as a prestigious world power.

Mussolini's ambitious plan was to cross the Egyptian border and rush east across to the Suez Canal in

A British soldier walks alongside a trainload of Italian prisoners who are delighted to be captured; the war is over for them. Since escape is the last thing on their minds, a single British soldier armed with only a pistol seems more than adequate. In less than two months, during late 1940 and early 1941, the British captured 130,000 Italian soldiers. *National Archives*

the same way the Germans blitzkrieged across Europe. While his motivation was a revival of the ancient days of Rome, the archaic weapons and methods he equipped his army with were also ancient history. Mussolini chose Marshal Rodolfo Graziani to lead his forces. Together, *Il Duce* and Graziani planned an offensive that would have been right at home during World War I, not in 1940s warfare.

The Italians did not simply fail to achieve their objectives. The British crushed them in one of the biggest routs of World War II. Overwhelmed in every conceivable way, the Italians were pushed backward and lost almost an entire army in the process. In two months, 130,000 Italian troops were captured. Adding to the humiliation was the fact that the Italians vastly outnumbered the British—more Italian soldiers were concentrated in Cyrenaica (a northeast region of Libya) than the British had stationed in the entire Middle East. Obsolete equipment of World War I vintage, old-fashioned methods, and inept leadership led to defeat after defeat.

As the Italians did an about-face and began a full retreat westward, British Lieutenant General Richard Nugent O'Connor wanted to ride the momentum of his advance past the Gulf of Sirte and into Tripoli, where the Italians were fleeing for refuge. This was the last important port the Italians held in North Africa and represented their only hope of resupply or retreat. But, incredibly, instead of finishing off the impotent Italian forces and booting them out of North Africa altogether, the British leadership pulled the plug on its victorious Mobile Desert Force as it was closing in on Benghazi, which would have been the last stop before the lunge into Tripolitania.

O'Connor's superior, Field Marshal Sir Archibald Wavell, stated, "The Italians in Tripolitania can be disregarded." Essentially, he was right. What remained were decimated elements of the X Italian Infantry

The face of quiet confidence. Rommel was ready for anything when he arrived in Berlin for a briefing on February 6, 1941. By the conclusion of the day, he understood the daunting but dazzling prospects that awaited him as commander in North Africa. Soon after, Rommel wrote excitedly to his wife: "You can imagine how my head is buzzing because of all these new developments. What will come of it?" *National Archives*

Corps, consisting of the Brescia, Pavia, and Bologna Divisions, as well as a small part of the Ariete Division. The bulk of the Ariete Armored Division was just arriving in Tripoli as the rest of the corps was retreating into the city. This decisive Italian defeat and the British decision not to destroy the remaining Fascist force occurred just five days before Rommel's arrival.

The Stage Is Set for Rommel

Rommel reported to the German High Command in Berlin on the morning of February 6, 1941, for a briefing with the army's commander-in-chief, Field Marshal Walther von Brauchitsch, and Hitler himself. Here, Rommel teetered on the brink of his destiny. With this assignment, an everyday soldier would be plucked from relative obscurity and thrust into a wide-open, free-wheeling setting that would showcase his genius.

He listened quietly and intently about the situation in North Africa. Von Brauchitsch prefaced the briefing with an overview of the Italians' desperate situation, the domination of British forces, and the recent history of Hitler's interactions with Mussolini. And finally, the course of action Germany would take. Operation *Sonnenblume* (Sunflower), was the code word for the intervention of German forces in North Africa.

What awaited him in von Brauchitsch's briefcase was a mixed bag of delight and disappointment. He was presented the official set of orders that appointed him corps commander in Africa. This likely sent a flush of anticipation through him. Then there was a pregnant pause when he heard where he would fit in the chain of command—subordinate to the *Italian* commander, Marshal Graziani.

Generally, the Italian command was viewed with disdain. German officers had long harbored the feeling that Italian officers were arrogant and ineffectual puppets of weak-minded dictator Benito Mussolini. Furthermore, they were masters over an ill-trained, ill-equipped, demoralized army.

From the Italian point of view, the intervention of German forces was not entirely welcomed. It was an embarrassment that their Axis big brother, Germany, would have to step in and fight the battle they weren't capable of fighting.

In fact, just a few months previous, during November 1940, Hitler had offered a panzer division to supplement Italian armor in Africa. The offer was at first accepted and then refused. It turned out that Mussolini had not wanted to share his "inevitable victory" over the British.

Hitler was sensitive to this humbling situation faced by his Italian ally, so he agreed to a chain of command that retained an Italian as overall chief in the North African Theater. That arrangement introduced unending complexities, both diplomatic and tactical.

Von Brauchitsch said the forces under Rommel's command would be known as *Deutsches Afrika Korps* or German Africa Corps. Thus, inside the Wehrmacht, the Afrika Korps was generally referred to by its German abbreviation, DAK. Hitler himself chose the name.

It consisted initially of two German divisions: The Fifth Panzer and Fifth Light. The vanguard of both divisions would be gradually augmented to full strength by May 1941.

The integrity of these divisions was not to be violated. In other words, the German units were not to be broken apart and deployed piecemeal to shore up elements of the fragmented Italian army. They would remain intact as German units.

Even though Rommel reported to the Italian commander-in-chief, he was allowed to short-circuit the chain of command and, in fact, was specifically instructed to go directly to Hitler if an order handed down from the Italian command seemed to compromise the integrity of the German units or their objective. This same order to bypass the Italian command was given to *Fliegerkorps X* air units under Reichmarshal Hermann Goering. The Germans had seen how the Italians had bungled operations in Greece, Italian Somaliland, Abyssinia, and, most of all, Libya. They weren't about

General Rommel, accompanied by Italian commander Italo Gariboldi, inspects a formation of German troops newly arrived from Europe in February 1941. Their winter-pale faces will soon become weathered by the merciless sun and wind of the desert. *National Archives*

German troops
unload water cans
in the meager
shade afforded by
a palm tree at a
small oasis.
National Archives

The age-old symbol of the desert, the palm tree, is adopted as the emblem of the Afrika Korps. The swastika superimposed on the palm tree adorns all Afrika Korps vehicles, as seen on the door of this truck. The scene also captures a common sight in the highly mobile desert war, as this two-wheel drive truck needs a four-wheel drive vehicle with chains to pull it free of the sand. *National Archives*

to tarnish their own military reputation by intermingling their soldiers with those of the Italians.

But at this time, the Afrika Korps as a fighting force had no reputation of its own. It had not existed as a unit before. It had not proven itself in the blitzkrieg across Europe and been shipped intact to fight as a unit in North Africa. Also, it was not conceived or thought of as an elite task force.

True, many of its troops were motivated veterans of the battles in Poland and France, but they had been drawn from various units across the Wehrmacht, so the range of experience was wide. They were not by any means handpicked by Rommel or Hitler, and certainly not specially trained for desert combat. They were soldiers from units designed to fight in Europe, and they could just as easily have been reassigned to units headed toward Russia, Norway, or the Netherlands.

But the Afrika Korps eventually became an elite force. Eberhard Ladwig alluded to this special nature in Carlson's *We Were Each Other's Prisoners:* "I was put in the infantry. A friend and I applied to the Afrika Korps, and we were the only two from the whole company who were accepted. The rest went to the Russian Front."

Prior to 1941, no Wehrmacht unit bore the Afrika Korps' distinctive symbol of a swastika superimposed on a palm tree. No military researchers had studied

A stark view over a soldier's cap. *Here is what the Afrika Korps soldiers saw as they left the relative paradise of Tripoli for their desert adventure. Signs of civilization became fewer and fewer as they wheeled inland, until Arabian dwellings like these were few and far between.*
National Archives

desert conditions. No specific training existed for desert combat, let alone desert survival. The men of the Afrika Korps had to learn as they went along.

The first waves of German troops to arrive in Tripoli had to assemble in formation and stand sweltering in the heavy woolen continental uniforms of the Wehrmacht. Benefiting from that most elementary of lessons, quartermasters issued a light tropical uniform to later arrivals before they left Germany.

Wehrmacht units had not been prepared for desert warfare simply because North Africa was not a planned theater of operations for Germany. This is surprising, considering the region's obvious strategic value. But Hitler did not view the southern Mediterranean as a priority, particularly in comparison to Operation Sea Lion, the invasion of Great Britain. The African intervention was simply to aid an Axis ally.

At the conclusion of this information-packed briefing, Rommel knew where he stood in the larger landscape of the war. It was a difficult assignment with many uncertainties and few assurances.

Preparing for this new adventure, he packed his bags with the barest necessities and wrote cryptically to his wife about going to a place for rheumatism treatment, which was a tip-off about where he was being sent. Before the war, Frau Rommel knew his doctor had recommended he go to the Egyptian desert, as a cure for his ailments.

He was being inserted into an unknown world that was almost as challenging as being ordered to do battle on the moon. Rommel faced severe desert conditions, where his equipment was untested and his troops untried. It was a delicate diplomatic arena, yet he knew his strength was not diplomacy. And he would have to fight an enemy whose strength was thought to be overwhelming.

Arrival in Africa

At noon on February 12, 1941, a Heinkel 111 bomber-transport carrying Erwin Rommel touched down for the first time on African soil at the Castel Benito airfield near Tripoli. Just as the plane rolled to a stop, a German liaison officer raced up to meet him. The lieutenant carried news that was not encouraging. The Italian retreat had turned into an "every-man-for-himself" flight to the west. The lieutenant reported,

Lashed to the deck of a transport ship are German 88-millimeter guns and vehicles bound for North Africa. Note the German soldiers behind the Kubelwagen are seated at a table and playing cards to pass the time, while another man is "traveling by rail"—a typical pose of landlubbers enduring the Mediterranean's rough seas. *National Archives*

A Panzer III medium tank, weighing about 20 tons, is hoisted off the deck for unloading at Tripoli. The Panzer III had a top speed of between 20 and 25 miles per hour and a unrefueled range of over 90 miles. Equipped with a 50-millimeter gun, its shells could penetrate British armor at 1,000 yards. *Rommelarchiv*

"Italian troops have thrown away their weapons and ammunition and clambered on to overloaded vehicles in a wild attempt to get away." This, along with an intelligence report telling of superior enemy strength in Tobruk, Benghazi, and the rest of Cyrenaica, painted a grim picture of the African battlefront.

Rommel noted in his diary: "Most of the Italian officers had already packed their bags and were hoping for a quick return trip to Italy." Based on this information, Rommel naturally had to assume the British would press on, carried by the momentum of their successful offensive, as O'Connor wanted to. In the first of countless bold and decisive moves he would make in the African Theater, Rommel wasted no time in determining his first step: In the absence of battle-ready troops and armor in force, he had to erect a facade of strength to buy time until his German troops arrived. This required Italian troops to be reorganized and redeployed from Tripoli east to the Gulf of Sirte. (Many of these soldiers had just spent days fleeing across hundreds of miles of desert.)

Italian soldiers stride through the streets of Tripoli. If they're smiling because they think they've won a ticket home to Italy after successfully fleeing from the British, they're wrong. Just as hordes of Italian soldiers finished a grueling retreat over hundreds of desert miles, Rommel met them with marching orders to turn around and take up defensive positions 250 miles east on the Gulf of Sirte. *National Archives*

The picture of power. This early Nazi propaganda photo is intended to show the superiority of the German soldier and his equipment. Provincial natives in flowing robes stand behind the tank while the Panzer III's commander strikes an erect, gallant posture. *National Archives*

New arrivals for the Afrika Korps from Europe await their orders on the dock. They wouldn't wait long. Rommel immediately sent all arriving units from the 5th Light Division to the Gulf of Sirte. *National Archives*

Rommel explained, "As the first German division would not be complete in Africa until the middle of April, its help would come too late if the enemy continued his offensive. Something had to be done at once to bring the British offensive to a halt."

With this deft assessment in hand, Rommel sought to report to his new immediate superior, Marshal Graziani. However, just before Rommel's arrival the Italian commander-in-chief had submitted his resignation to Italian King Victor Emmanuel III. Graziani was succeeded by General Italo Gariboldi, then 62 years old.

Already at 1 P.M., Rommel was meeting with the newly appointed commander-in-chief to discuss his plan. Gariboldi emphatically disagreed with him. (Barely an hour after his arrival in Africa, Rommel had this first of many disagreements and struggles with Gariboldi. He would have more with Gariboldi's eventual successor, General Ettore Bastico, during the coming two years.) The Italian commander was convinced that a defensive posture just outside Tripoli was the only logical strategy.

His disrespect barely concealed, Rommel left the meeting to fly an aerial reconnaissance in his He 111 over Sirte, a small village on the coast east of Tripoli. The flight confirmed his instincts. He observed that a "belt of sand" ringed Tripoli with a natural obstacle for tracked vehicles. This meant that the Gulf of Sirte was the right place to take up a defensive position.

Before he landed in Tripoli that evening, he resolved to follow through on his plan and also to assume tactical command of the troops sent to this new front. He would deploy the troops at Sirte, which was located on the shores of the Mediterranean, halfway between Tripoli and El Agheila, the port city where the British finally halted their pursuit.

This decision showed Rommel was more than confident. Remember that he was a German general, in an Italian theater, with less than a day on site, and technically no troops of his own to command. Somehow, after meeting once more with Gariboldi, Rommel emerged with command of the front, and an approved order for Italian troops of the Ariete Division to be dispatched to Sirte.

The panic-stricken Italian troops were still streaming westward into Tripoli, only to be met now by their new commander Rommel, who bullied them into marching 250 miles in the opposite direction. Observing the ragtag columns, Rommel wrote: "Morale was as low as it could be in all military circles in Tripoli."

Within two days, on February 14, the first German troops landed in force at Tripoli. Elements of the

A Bussing-NAG Sd.Kfz half-track, destined for Rommel's armored divisions, is lowered to Tripoli's dock. Thousands found use in the desert sands as a personnel carriers and artillery tractors. *Rommelarchiv*

Two Luftwaffe airmen adopt the common North African household pet, a monkey. *Rommelarchiv*

An Africa Korps soldier
with the original "ship of the desert," the one-humped Arabian camel. **Rommelarchiv**

5th Light Division, which included a reconnaissance battalion and an antitank battalion, were the first to arrive. Rommel risked aerial attack by unloading his men under the bright lights of Tripoli's port; but in doing so, he had the two battalions positioned on the front lines at Sirte within 26 hours.

As the days passed without the British continuing their offensive, Rommel began to get suspicious. Intelligence reports, reconnaissance probes on the ground, and Rommel's own aerial reconnaissance began to uncover the truth about British strength in Africa. The descriptions of enemy strength initially reported to him when he landed at Tripoli on February 12 were no longer accurate and, in fact, were out of date on the day he arrived.

British troops were being redeployed from Africa to shore up Greek defenses in the face of a combined Italian-German invasion. Rommel was not privy to that plan when he met with von Brauchitsch and Hitler on February 6. But even if he had been, none of them could have known for certain what ramifications the invasion would have on British forces in Africa, or that it would give Rommel a brief window of opportunity to reorganize the Axis forces in North Africa and form plans to strike eastward.

Awaiting Opposition: The British

British Commonwealth forces in Africa comprised men from England, Australia, and New

continued on page 37

Axis forces in a formal ceremony in North Africa. The German and Italian flags fly over an old fort in Tripolitania. *Rommelarchiv*

Two British M3 light tanks blaze a trail across the desert. Formally named the (General) Stuart tank, it was popularly known as the "Honey" in North Africa. Maneuverable and quick, it was powered by a radial seven-cylinder gasoline engine. *National Archives*

Military regulations for uniforms and hygiene are quickly dispensed with once in the field. Some remnants of the tropical-issue uniform, designed by Hamburg's Tropical Institute, are retained by these soldiers. But the pith helmet and certainly the khaki necktie of the original uniform are immediately discarded. Boots, either ankle or knee-high, become the choice of the wearer. The original issue of tunics and breeches have been exchanged for the olive-green, lightweight cotton shorts and shirts, that are similar to or, in some cases, virtually the same as the British desert uniform (gained from raids on British supply depots). All soldiers also are issued great coats for the desert's frigid nights. *National Archives*

Resembling an Egyptian mummy, this German soldier wears a standard issue mask and goggles to shield his face from blinding, stinging sand and choking dust. *Bundesarchiv*

Early soldiers of the Afrika Korps,

still clean-shaven in pith helmets and regulation uniforms, and equipped with standard Mauser infantry rifles. Their pith helmets, initially standard issue to all desert troops, will soon be replaced by steel helmets and soft-billed caps. National Archives

Continued from page 32

Zealand, as well as some Nepalese Gurkhas, Indian Sikhs, and Jewish and Polish troops who had escaped the German blitzkrieg in eastern Europe. When the Italians had been beaten to the point that British leaders felt they no longer posed a threat, and Germany began to mass its forces for an invasion of Greece, the British Cabinet transferred much of the Commonwealth force out of North Africa in early 1941. This grave mistake would prolong the desert war for two bloody years.

Under orders from Churchill, Wavell snatched most of the experienced commanders and battle-hardened combat soldiers from their position on the Axis doorstep. Most were diverted to Greece to fulfill Churchill's promise to protect that country from Axis occupation. Others were sent to eastern Africa or back to Great Britain. Only a minimal defensive force stood fast in Cyrenaica: The 9th Australian Division and part of the 2nd Armored Division.

Although their front-line troops were largely new and inexperienced, the British had a definite edge in the larger context of desert warfare knowledge. In sharp contrast to the inexperience of the Germans

Sweltering heat and wind makes scarce water the singular most essential substance for all living beings in the desert. The ration was usually one gallon per man per day for *all* his needs. Rommel was an avid amateur photographer, he's known to have taken this photo himself, and several others in this book. *National Archives*

A German doctor administers inoculations to soldiers soon after their arrival. Most soldiers had no experience dealing with the wide variety of diseases and parasites facing them in North Africa. *National Archives*

(who had never fought in desert conditions), the British had decades of combat experience in the Middle East. They had fought the Turks in Egypt and Palestine during World War I. During the 1920s, British colonial forces experimented with military maneuvers in the desert. In 1936, when Italian forces crossed the border of Cyrenaica to invade Ethiopia, the British deployed their Mobile Desert Force—the first modern desert fighting unit—to guard British interests. Their desert warfare experience was a contributing reason why, for 14 months since early December 1940, their considerably smaller forces had been thrashing the Italians.

But the architect of that thrashing, the brilliant tactician O'Connor, was now out of action—ailing from months in battle and desert conditions. Lieutenant General Sir Maitland Wilson assumed command briefly in early February, but he also was ordered to Greece. Wilson was followed by Lieutenant General Sir Philip Neame.

A crew from an engineering unit *drills a well near Tripoli. Finding water to stay alive in the desert was one of the constant challenges for the Afrika Korps.* National Archives

Water drawn from desert wells is boiled thoroughly before it is poured into water cans that will be transported to soldiers in the field. *National Archives*

Under Neame's orders, British forces were spread thin and scattered. Parts of the remaining divisions were dug in at Mersa el Brega, near El Agheila. Two Australian brigades remained at positions northeast of Benghazi. The remaining troops were far to the rear. Despite the protests of subordinate commanders, Neame felt the dispersion was appropriate.

Based on his personal reconnaissance flights, Rommel knew about the dispersal of British troops. They had not yet fortified their positions, but Rommel knew it would only be a short time before they did. With British troops scattered and unsuspecting, he concluded his small forces could match them. He pinpointed a position from Mersa el Brega south to Bir es Suera as his immediate tactical objective—the first step in the offensive he envisioned.

He realized the Italian troops were in no condition to attack. But he knew that with each passing week his German tank and troop strength would grow. Soon, he could launch his first major assault on British defenses in North Africa.

The Desert as a Battlefield

The Libyan Desert, also known as the Western Desert, would become Rommel's domain. Although one of the harshest environments on Earth for man and machine, the desert's barren vastness presented the perfect setting for a master of military maneuver.

Under the earth's broadest sky lies an endless panorama of achromatic plateaus and parched banks of sand dunes. In Richard Lidz's oral history, *Many Kinds of Courage*, there is an apt description of this land: "We had an expression in the desert, 'going up the blue,' or 'being in the blue,' because you had just a vast dome of blue sky touching the horizons north, south, east and west." Gerard Hacquebard, a twice-wounded veteran of Grenadier Guards, is quoted in Lidz's book as saying, "I was always amazed at the openness of the western desert, which seemed to reach for miles and miles."

The pervasive features of the Western Desert are jagged shelves of bare rock, where capricious winds have stripped away sand, clay, and dirt. Dried-out riverbeds, called *wadis*, with cracked soil bottoms and

Any shade, manmade or natural, is sought. Here, soldiers clean their rifles before the launch of Rommel's campaign into Cyrenaica. *National Archives*

The living is Spartan, but water is not the only drink. On occasion, the delicacy of Italian wine is available and sold directly from the barrel. *National Archives*

not a trace of moisture, are common, as are bleached animal bones, sand that sparkles with tiny jewels of white gypsum, searing heat, unimpeded wind, and most of all, the relentless sun.

The cloudless sky of North Africa allows about 3,000 hours of sunshine each year. The intensity of the light seems to make the barren landscape shimmer and sway. It cruelly tricks the eye into believing a welcoming cool pond or a shady oasis lies just ahead—then it fades into nothingness.

Temperatures as high as 136 degrees Fahrenheit in the shade have been recorded here. Yet nighttime temperatures can frequently drop to below freezing.

The winds seem to rise up from hell itself. Blast furnace-like gusts whip up grit from the desert floor with such fury that it becomes nearly impossible to breathe or see. Grains of sand pelt the skin. Faces become chapped. Lips crack. Wind-propelled grit penetrates sealed compasses and wristwatches, and cuts the

normal operating life of engines in half. It even strips the paint from trucks and tanks. The winds of the desert, personified with names like Sirocco and Haboob, hit with all the ferocity of an enemy attack.

To quote Hacquebard in *Many Kinds of Courage*, "If you fired your artillery or rifles during a sandstorm, the breeches would stick and the rifling in the barrel would seize up . . . During a sandstorm, all you do is sit tight, lie still, cover your face and your head, and wish it were over."

Rommel's German troops had never seen anything like this. It would be up to him to whip his corps into a fighting force capable of facing the desert, and the British army. Soon after his arrival, Rommel ordered a training course to be set up on a sandy peninsula on the Baltic, in an attempt to simulate Western Desert conditions. Afrika Korps recruits slept in sweat-box barracks, overheated to acclimate them. Enormous fans kicked up blinding dust during training.

Springtime in particular is known for violent wind

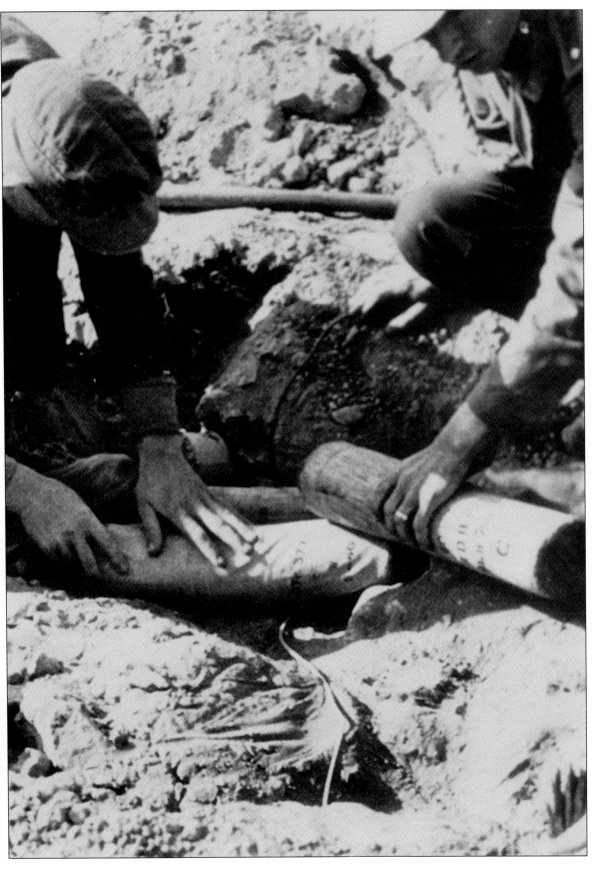

Explosive charges are placed into solid rock to blast a hole for a gun emplacement. In some parts of the desert, the layer of sand is extremely deep and easy to burrow into; in other places, there is no more than a thin veneer of dust over solid rock. *National Archives*

Digging trenches is almost a daily need, given the constant movement of mobile warfare. Burrowing beneath the ground affords some protection from enemy attack and the ravages of extreme temperatures and wind. *National Archives*

In the interior of North Africa, their faces dripped with sweat and the fine dust of the desert adhered to their skin, making every man appear a jaundiced yellow. The combination of sweat and dust became a viscous paste, making the soldiers' hair as stiff as a plastic action figure. Once this effect set in, it lasted as long as the trooper was "in country," since showers were nonexistent.

There were few developed roads in Libya except the Via Balbia, built by Italian engineers along the coast. However, in most places the desert floor provided a firm surface for tanks to traverse. Movement was almost as free as a fleet at sea. In fact, the land to the south of the Mediterranean shore was called "the Great Sand Sea."

Like other desert tacticians, Rommel saw the analogy between desert warfare and a naval battle. Both desert and sea are trackless, uncharted expanses navigated best by stars, sun, and sextant. There were no towns, no rivers, nor any cities or dwellings to guide, inhibit, or shelter the Afrika Korps, nor was there any civilian population to be endangered by battle.

The desert truly was "a tactician's paradise and a quartermaster's hell," which was a popular phrase at the time. Because there was virtually no food or water to be found that would sustain an army in the field, supply lines were the only tether that limited movement. Rommel's relentless offensives drove ever farther into enemy territory, straining against that tether.

Once beyond the mountains, traveling further to the south, there is a subtle change in the earth. The surface passing by is the same monotonous, dun color. What's different is beneath the surface. In the north, great tables of rock are covered with a thin veneer of

A sign for a German truck repair depot: *Instandsetzungs-Kompanie* or "Inst. Komp," indicates a rear echelon unit designated 2/200. This company was tasked with the overhaul, service and repair of Afrika Korps vehicles. *National Archives*

storms in the Libyan Desert. During the first Cyrenaica offensive in the spring of 1941, this is what awaited Rommel's troops beyond the coastal mountain range that serves as a picturesque backdrop for Tripoli, Libya's capital and a main deep water port.

When they first landed, the troops of the Afrika Korps were impressed with the climate and setting. But this was Tripoli, the "crown jewel of Italy's colonies." It had modern buildings, and palm tree-shadowed streets to accent the lush green seaside. The mountains keep Mediterranean clouds and their life-giving moisture from passing south, creating a sharp juxtaposition between the coastal lands and the arid and barren countryside that awaited the German troops. They soon received a strong dose of reality.

Maintenance of vehicles

is critical for a mobile desert war. With the extreme heat, close monitoring of radiators is a must and the need to clean filters choked by penetrating dust is constant. Here men carry containers of water to the vehicles. The precious water has probably already been used for washing and shaving.

National Archives

sand. The rock made it nearly impossible for troops to dig even shallow trenches there. Further south, the sand (actually powdery dust) gets deeper and softer, so that digging trenches is easy, but driving vehicles, especially anything with tires, was very tricky and sometimes impossible.

The North African battlefield was vast. The northernmost boundary was the shore of the Mediterranean Sea and, while there was no clear southern boundary, the battlefield ranged roughly 150 miles inland. Its breadth extended from Tripoli a distance of more 1,500 miles east to El Alamein. This was in excess of 200,000 square miles of parched landscape that, in the words of German writer and Afrika Korps chronicler Paul Carrell, "could absorb a great quantity of blood."

Ancient cisterns and tombs, dotting the blank countryside, were among the only manmade features. The one clearly dominating natural feature that served to frame one side of the wasteland was a 500-foot escarpment, facing north to the coastal plain. An escarpment is a steep slope separating two relatively flat plateaus of different elevations. This escarpment was a cliff falling by ledges to the sea, like giant stair steps. It was impassable to wheeled vehicles, except through a few gaps and passes. These areas became highly prized and necessary for mobile operations. Halfaya Pass, later to become the scene of a great battle, was one of those strategic passes.

Only a few living creatures enter and endure the habitat of the desert. Spiders, scarab-like beetles, biting flies and fleas are numerous. There are also scorpions

This circular machine gun emplacement has been carved out of the sand and subterranean rock. The desert presented a wide-open field of fire, so the circular trench allowed the gunner to fire in all directions. *National Archives*

Desert warfare ravages vehicles,
but this repair had nothing to do with battle damage. Here, a Kubelwagen, built on the
standard Volkswagen chassis, undergoes repair for common drive-train problems in the desert. At top left, the
rear axle needs replacing; just above, the front suspension needs repair. In the upper right, a line up of disabled
Kubelwagens await mechanics at a repair company depot. National Archives

Makeshift methods were necessary. Here a cloth sleeve (literally a sleeve off a uniform tunic) is wrapped around an engine pipe and sealed with wire on each end—anything to help keep out the fine sand that can penetrate everything and grind moving parts to a halt. *National Archives*

One BMW R75 (750-cc) motorcycle is cannibalized to bring another back to life. The Afrika Korps initially had an entire motorcycle battalion—the 15th Battalion—which was later absorbed into other units. The mission of Rommel's motorcyclists was to dart through gaps in the enemy lines for reconnaissance. *National Archives*

so venomous that their sting can kill you in only four hours, poisonous snakes and lizards, jackals and rats—even an occasional herd of gazelles. And, the world's smallest fox, the fennec. This fox is recognizable by ears enormous in proportion to its head and body. It is uniquely suited to the desert for the way it radiates away heat through its ears, which helps it retain water that would be lost by panting.

The Desert Fox himself, Erwin Rommel, found he too was uniquely suited to the conditions of the desert. And he made the most of what he had. To the astonishment of everyone, including the British and the German-Italian command, he would win stunning victories against his adversaries in the days that followed his arrival in North Africa.

Chapter Three

TRIUMPH
AGAINST THE ODDS— AND AGAINST ORDERS

Rommel was not content to assume a defensive posture. Soon after his arrival in North Africa, he set out on the offensive, despite the mission dictated by his superiors. When he realized there was a fleeting chance to exploit the weakened British army, he didn't hesitate.

And "consternation" did result. The Italian High Command was angry. The German High Command was angry. Von Brauchitsch was vocal, calling it "insubordination of such proportions." And Albert Speer, always an insider to Hitler, recounted in his memoirs, *Inside the Third Reich*: "[Hitler] was bitterly annoyed with Rommel, who would often give extremely unclear bulletins on the day's movements. In other words, he 'veiled' them from headquarters, sometimes for days, only to report an entirely changed situation. Hitler liked Rommel personally but could ill brook this sort of conduct."

> *"There'll be consternation among our masters in Tripoli and Rome, perhaps in Berlin too. I took the risk against all orders and instructions because the opportunity seemed favorable."*
>
> — Letter to Lu
> April 3, 1941

Rommel was a good soldier, and good soldiers obey orders. But the justification in Rommel's own mind for his conduct in Africa was this: The vantage point of Berlin did not give as clear a picture as he had on the front lines.

Blunders of British Command

It was partly their history of colonialism and flawed logic over occupied territory that led to the British decision not to press on to Tripoli and vanquish the remaining Italian forces. The old conventional wisdom of warfare told the British that they had gone far enough and occupied a key geographic area, featuring the prized port at Tobruk. But stopping short left the enemy alive and capable of striking back.

Just before the British capture of Tobruk, Field Marshal Smuts, the prime minister of the Union of South Africa, sent a telegram to Churchill that said: "Flowing tide will soon carry Wavell to Tobruk. Should he go further? Tripoli

Rommel rides with General Italo Gariboldi (right) during a visit to Italian and German units. Many Italian commanders, like Gariboldi, were accustomed to safe and relatively plush accommodations in the rear, while their soldiers lived a punishing life on the frontier. Rommel's style was to live up front with the troops, which he expected of his subordinate commanders as well. *National Archives*

is much too far. Even Benghazi is as far beyond the frontier as the frontier is from Alexandria . . . in the absence of good and special reasons Tobruk seems to me the terminus."

The essence of Smuts' recommendation was that there were unnecessary risks in going on to Tripolitania to boot out the Italians from North Africa once and for all. He felt that the British should instead set up defenses for the territory they now held.

O'Connor was allowed to push just past the coastal city of Benghazi to El Agheila and was told to stop. Churchill then gleefully cabled Smuts on February 15, to say that the capture of "Benghazi, Cyrenaica, gives us a secure flank for Egypt." Now, the priority for British forces would be directed elsewhere.

But this left the remaining Italian forces intact and in control of Tripoli, where the door was opened wide for its port to welcome Rommel and his Afrika Korps.

Other British command blunders were more understandable, like the assumption that the newly arrived

German forces in Tripoli were not well prepared to mount a quick offensive. If Churchill himself had been in Hitler's office when von Brauchitsch issued the directives to Rommel for his African assignment, Churchill would not have changed his orders to Wavell. After all, Rommel was explicitly ordered to take a defensive stance in protection of the Italian allies.

In addition, Wavell's staff was supremely confident that any attack on Cyrenaica could be thwarted by the topography of the escarpment and British defenses at the passes. All odds seemed in their favor. Confident in their position in Africa, Churchill and his War Cabinet turned their attention back to the defense of Greece.

But there was one variable—an incalculable force—in the equation: Erwin Rommel.

Early Action

The Afrika Korps' first recorded skirmish with British forces happened on February 24, 1941. It was a minor encounter when a hapless British reconnaissance patrol of the King's Dragoon Guards encountered elements of the German 3rd Reconnaissance Battalion. The result—no German casualties and three British POWs.

Early encounters like this had Rommel thirsting for an offensive. He sought permission to strike immediately, but von Brauchitsch flatly refused. The German commander reminded Rommel that no major offensive was planned for North Africa and that no more troops (other than those promised at the initial briefing) would be forthcoming. Rommel again was not made privy to other, larger plans that would draw German resources into shoring up Italian forces foundering in Greece, as well as Hitler's titanic plan to invade Russia.

Still, Rommel could not ignore the obvious vulnerability of British forces. He resolved to capitalize on their weakness at the first possible moment.

Meanwhile, his own forces were gathering strength steadily. The 5th Panzer Regiment with 120 tanks arrived on March 11. In total, he had 166 German tanks. From the Italians, he inherited 60 obsolete tanks, better known as "mobile coffins."

Italian forces were being redeployed and supplemented. By mid-March, the Italian Brescia Division took position at the El Mugtaa line, which allowed the German 5th Light Division to come off the line and prepare for an offensive.

Through February and March, a profusion of supplies came streaming into Tripoli—a luxury the Afrika Korps would not enjoy regularly as their campaign continued. Of the 220,000 tons shipped during those first two months, 200,000 tons arrived safely and only 20,000 tons were sent to the bottom of the Mediterranean by the Royal Navy and RAF. Such proportions became flip-flopped during the lean months to follow, when Malta-based aircraft and naval forces ravaged Axis transports and cargo ships.

Deceptions to Fool the Allies

Rommel was still worried that the British would attack before his forces were prepared. To intimidate the enemy, he did not try to keep the buildup of his forces a secret. In fact, he used the tactics of a blowfish to seem bigger than he was.

One of hundreds of fake tanks that made up Rommel's "Cardboard Division" in the spring of 1941. Rommel's objective was to fool British reconnaissance pilots into thinking he already had substantial armored strength when, in reality, his panzer divisions arrived piecemeal throughout the winter and spring. The ruse worked. From a distance, the "tanks" (made of plywood, canvas, and sawed-off telegraph poles for barrels mounted on Volkswagen or Fiat chassis) looked real. *National Archives*

A Panzer III of the 5th Light Division newly arrived in Tripoli in February 1941.
Rommelarchiv

A truck carrying Italian troops rumbles across one of the engineering innovations of the Via Balbia coastal roadway, a barrel bridge. It is the handiwork of engineers who made a roadway using discarded petroleum barrels to cross terrain that otherwise would have been impassable. *National Archives*

To create the illusion of strength for his adversarial audience, he ordered the fabrication of over 200 phony tanks and armored cars. These were actually Volkswagens and some Fiats covered with canvas, wood and anything else available to suggest steel turrets and armor. Wooden poles were sawed into barrel lengths and mounted to look like guns. This was Rommel's "Cardboard Division," parked in staging areas and intended for the eyes of RAF reconnaissance pilots. To reinforce the illusion, real tanks crisscrossed the sandy plateaus to create a huge network of tracks (begging notice from reconnaissance pilots) as if hundreds of tanks made them.

Knowing that Allied eyes would be watching, Rommel shamelessly paraded his units through Tripoli, as if proudly displaying the might of his armor to boost the morale of the beleaguered Italians. In reality, it was part of a deceptive plan to convince any Allied spies who might be watching (and in Tripoli, some no doubt were) that a formidable German force was already in North Africa. At the time, he had a small armored column. The vehicles drove through Tripoli's town square, then at the east end of town turned and looped back to reenter on the west end. They paraded through again and again in what appeared to be an infinite armada.

On March 25, 1941, Rommel massed his forces at dawn in full view of the British. He chose to do this at El Agheila, an old, dilapidated fort near the El Mugtaa line. It was also the westernmost position of the British Western Desert Force. Rommel moved his armor into position for what presumably was to be a full frontal assault. At the same time he dispatched two columns of the Volkswagen and Fiat "tanks" (at a safe distance to maintain the illusion) to straddle the outpost. Faced with the prospect of being outnumbered threefold or more, the British withdrew.

This was the first of many examples in Africa in which Rommel's constant readiness for change and fluidity was precisely right for the situation at hand. On a moment's notice, as opportunity presented itself, Rommel seized it. He would not order a British-style consolidation and set up a defensive position at El Agheila. Rommel moved on.

Rommel's First Cyrenaican Campaign

The first large-scale battle began at 9:50 A.M. on March 31, 1941. The date was remarkable since Rommel had arrived only six weeks before and his units were arriving piecemeal during the time in between.

Frequent reconnaissance flights had told him much about the situation that awaited the Afrika Korps. Forty miles east of El Agheila, the British had set up a defensive line that extended from the sea south through Mersa el Brega. Rommel's first thought was to make a flank attack. But he found that dipping south in order to skirt the stronger frontal defenses was not an option, because the terrain there (mostly sand and salt marshes) was terrible for mechanized travel.

After the show of force at El Agheila, the British were well aware of Rommel's intentions for advancing. They began beefing up their defenses with minefields and tank barriers. Deducing that a delay would allow the enemy to strengthen his position even more, Rommel made the command decision to strike immediately. Keep in mind that all this was happening while his superiors in Berlin and Rome *still* directed a defensive posture.

In what later came to be known as Rommel's first Cyrenaican campaign, elements of the 3rd Reconnaissance Battalion struck at forward posts manned by the British 2nd Support Group. When the reconnaissance probe was repelled, the 5th Panzer Regiment was

called in. However, British armor was deployed as well, and again the Germans were repelled.

Later that afternoon, with Stuka dive bombers in support, the 8th Machine Gun Battalion supplemented the attacking forces and broke through British defenses. Once across the lines, the Germans fought their way up to Mersa el Brega.

Wavell ordered Neame to withdraw. The old fortress of Mersa el Brega fell into German hands in late afternoon, yielding a booty of 50 Bren gun carriers and 30 trucks.

Wavell's plan was to fight delaying actions along 140 miles of curvy coastline northward and then take a firm stand at Benghazi. An additional order to Neame was to keep losses of his mechanized units to a minimum, because so much British armor had been diverted to operations elsewhere.

All along the Via Balbia, *signs warn German soldiers of minefields on both sides of the road.* National Archives

The bird's eye view from an aircraft reveals enemy positions. Rommel personally took innumerable flights over the desert terrain to get a firsthand look at enemy direction and numbers. Based on his own air reconnaissance, Rommel reached well-informed conclusions about British vulnerability, which led to his decision to launch an offensive on March 31, 1941. *National Archives*

Rommel plunged onward from Mersa el Brega directly to Agedabia, which he promptly surrounded, defused and bypassed.

Throughout these advances, Rommel was in the midst of the action, racing up and down his battle line in whatever vehicle was available, always relying on firsthand observation as the basis for his command decisions. This was in complete disregard of his personal safety.

There were numerous near-misses. In one low-level reconnaissance flight in a Fieseler Storch aircraft just beyond Agedabia, he was mistakenly fired on by Italian units. The plane, which resembled a Piper Cub (and had about as much protective armor) was hit, but Rommel came through without a scratch.

In the first week of April, the Afrika Korps barreled up the coast road. Rommel not only took Benghazi, but he blew past it like the Sirocco and seized Barce and Derna, all on a stubby peninsula that protruded out into the Mediterranean.

It was at Benghazi that Neame had been specifically ordered to halt Rommel's advance. However,

Rommel studies a map on the hood of his command car, while German and Italian unit commanders look on and await individual assignments. Rommel's plans were not based on tactics that would win him vast stretches of open territory; they were meant to vanquish his enemy. *National Archives*

Rommel meets with his German staff to finalize plans for an assault. *National Archives*

Tanks and other vehicles kick up powdery sand that can be seen for miles. Sometimes the clouds of dust were deliberate, as Rommel sought to give the Allies an impression of great numbers of tanks. He used the criss-cross of many tank tracks, seen from the air, to give the impression that a great force was near. *Rommelarchiv*

A column is on the move toward British positions. The closest vehicle in the foreground is a towed 88-millimeter antiaircraft gun adapted for use in the antitank role. *Rommelarchiv*

Tracked vehicles of the Italian Ariete Division approach a British position. *National Archives*

An unsettling look down the barrel of a Panzer. British troops at Mersa el Brega might have seen this view— only the German crewmen wouldn't have been looking so casual or flashing a smile. *National Archives*

Neame would not be around to face the wrath of Wavell over his failure. Later, in the desperation of trying to rally his failing troops, Neame, accompanied by O'Connor who had been sent back to advise him, took a wrong turn in their staff car and found themselves in the middle of a German column on the outskirts of Derna. Both generals were captured when their car was overtaken by a motorcycle detachment.

Again observing from his Storch, Rommel saw that the British were in the midst of a large-scale retreat. Plus, he knew they were now leaderless. While his Italo-German forces continued their sweep along the coast, he ordered some elements to split and traverse straight across the desert interior to head off the retreating enemy at Gazala. This was almost precisely a reversal of the pursuit that O'Connor had executed to capture thousands of Italians just a few months earlier.

"Dear Lu," he wrote on April 3, 1941, "I took the risk against all orders and instructions because the opportunity seemed favorable. . . . The British are falling over each other to get away. I can't sleep for happiness."

But not all went like clockwork as the British were "falling over each other to get away." During one of his countless reconnaissance flights, Rommel chose to land in the vicinity of Mechili, an inland village in the path of his forces that were sent to head off the British retreat. From the air, he had seen no troop movement nearby, friendly or otherwise. The Storch was known for its ability to take off and land on short stretches of rough and uneven terrain, but when it came time to leave, Rommel discovered the aircraft was mired in the loose sand of a dune and couldn't pull free. In the distance was the telltale swirling dust of approaching vehicles and a glance through binoculars revealed that it was a British column. With the good fortune that seemed to follow him everywhere throughout the campaign, he found an abandoned German truck nearby. He and his pilot managed to start the vehicle and speed away before the enemy was upon them.

Although he escaped, this close call had severed any sort of contact with his headquarters for several hours during a key juncture in the battle. During the advance, there was a brief period when it might have made sense to bypass Mechili for the time being and bring the reconsolidated forces to bear on Tobruk, a much greater prize. But Rommel was unable to communicate with his headquarters to stay apprised of the situation or modify orders as the battle developed.

Rommel stands in his command car, windows caked with sand, to observe firsthand the proceedings on the front lines. *National Archives*

His insistence on being so mobile—either traveling up and down the battle lines by car or in an aircraft for reconnaissance flights—was a double-edged sword. On one hand, there was no substitute for firsthand knowledge of the battle, giving him the ability to adjust his forces immediately to make the most of any situation. On the other hand, during the sporadic course of fast-moving tank warfare, it was inevitable that Rommel would be pinned down at times by enemy fire or lost or stranded. This left his forces without a commander—sometimes at a crucial moment.

On the whole, the first Cyrenaican offensive was astonishingly victorious. It left mouths gapping in London, and in Berlin and Rome. The high commands in all three capitals had believed that an offensive was not possible until May. There were strong words used (such as "dangerous lunatic") at the German High Command to describe Rommel. Hitler sent him a message advising restraint in the future. But Rommel could hardly be reprimanded for recovering Cyrenaica and rescuing the Italian ally.

In just five days, Rommel had pushed British forces out of western Cyrenaica. He exploited every opportunity that came his way. And still, as British divisions fell back, Rommel pursued.

British units and strongholds captured along the way meant captured supplies and equipment for the Germans. These served to further fuel Rommel's advance.

As the spoils of war were being tallied, Rommel himself inspected some of the captured British vehicles. Among them were three huge armored trucks, which he and his staff promptly dubbed *"Mammuts"* (mammoths in English). Actually, they were Dorchester command vehicles, which were large and angular and well protected by armor plate. Inside one of them, as he looked for maps and other helpful intelligence, he came across a pair of British Perspex (plastic) goggles intended specifically for desert use against sand and sun.

From that moment on, the *Mammut* and the Perspex goggles became inextricably tied to the image Rommel projected to the world. The general was most typically pictured with those goggles resting on the visor of his cap, while he stood high up on his new mobile headquarters in a commanding posture. It seemed ironic and fitting that Rommel now took his place in the commander's seat of an expropriated British armored vehicle. For now, incredibly, Rommel was in the driver's seat to control the whole of Libya.

First Attack on Tobruk

Located on a crescent-shaped bay, Tobruk was the best North African port between Alexandria, Egypt, and Sfax, Tunisia. For the Nazis, Tobruk was also the gateway to their eastern ambitions, because it could feed the advance onward into Egypt. Rommel knew it. The British knew it too, so they made Tobruk a deathtrap.

Before the British had captured the city a few months before, Tobruk had been in Italian hands for 30 years. It had been annexed, along with other parts of the African coast, by Italy in 1911, when the Balkan states went to war with Turkey. After Mussolini came to power in 1922, amenities like restaurants, offices, shops and a hotel were constructed. Most importantly, the port and naval base were expanded and defenses built up around the city. An antitank ditch and a double ring of concrete fortifications circled Tobruk.

The city's natural topography further aided in its defense—to the east and west were wadis too steep for tanks and other motorized vehicles to cross. All of the land defenses were designed to shield the harbor, leaving vulnerability only from sea and air.

After the capture of O'Connor and Neame, Wavell himself flew to Tobruk to get the situation under control. He ordered Australian generals Morshead and Lavarack to bolster the existing defenses and position forces at the passes into the city. Tobruk was the last bastion between Rommel and Cairo. It must not be lost.

On Wavell's return flight to Cairo, his plane had mechanical difficulties and made a forced landing in the desert. Like Rommel only a few days before,

Rommel and one of his staff officers keep close watch on the battle. Anxious to always have a clear vantage point on the battle, Rommel was constantly on the move with his troops. As a result, he directed and redirected his panzers, based on what he saw as the fight developed. *National Archives*

Wavell narrowly escaped an approaching enemy column. Wavell's good fortune came in the form of a single Sudanese soldier driving a truck. The driver happened upon his plane by incredible chance and whisked him to safety.

On April 10, 1941, the Afrika Korps skidded to a halt at the outer defenses of Tobruk. Rommel positioned his units for assault and, flushed with success over the past two weeks, he fully expected to slice through Tobruk's defenses like a hot knife through butter. But against three bloody German assaults, Tobruk held. Rather than being repulsed again, Rommel chose the option of bypassing Tobruk. However, it proved to be a questionable decision. Failure to capture

Their gun trained on the stretch of desert before them, German troops in early 1941 keep watch for the approaching British. *National Archives*

A temporary camp is set up alongside a Panzer III, which has been hastily camouflaged for protection from air attack while it sits stationary. *National Archives*

the city during this first sweep over the coast would leave a festering thorn in his side for eight months to come, and inhibit his momentum eastward toward the objective of Egypt.

Rommel pressed on 75 miles to just west of Sollum, where he decided to play it safe by setting up defenses. The British took up positions east. In the ever-aggressive style of Rommel's desert fighting, he ordered an attack a few days later and pushed through to Buq Buq. Finally, he was content with his position by the end of April, and defenses on both sides were reestablished and forces regrouped.

Operation Battleaxe

Operation Battleaxe was Wavell's master plan to overpower Rommel and recapture what was lost. It was the assault that Churchill had been hounding Wavell to execute since mid-April.

Expressly for the offensive, Churchill had given highest priority of military resources to North Africa and put the Royal Navy at considerable risk to get reinforcements to Wavell through the Axis-infested Mediterranean. The "Tiger Convoy," as it was called, delivered a profusion of troops, supplies, and tanks at Alexandria.

Wavell's units were substantially reinforced. The British 7th Armored Division, which had gone without any resupply of equipment since February, was fully refurbished with 240 tanks. He also was given the 4th Indian Division, in full fighting trim from a triumphant campaign against the Italians in Abyssinia. These two divisions tipped the balance of firepower considerably in favor of the British.

Rommel stands amidst a group of high-ranking Italian officers. This is a telling pose: One of Rommel's subordinates (far left) fulfills the diplomatic role of graciously greeting the Italians, while Rommel's back remains turned. The relationship between officers of the two nations was uneasy throughout the desert war. *National Archives*

Soldiers line up at the mess truck
to get dinner. Standard fare included black rye or wheat bread, sardines in olive oil, processed cheese in tubes, oatmeal gruel, hard biscuits, and dehydrated vegetables. When the RAF and Royal Navy regained domination of the Mediterranean, food became harder to come by and even this basic fare must have sounded appetizing. National Archives

Rommel eats with his soldiers in the field. For the groundpounder, it is infinitely comforting to know that your commander is putting up with the same rations as you. For Rommel, it paid great dividends in the form of boosted morale and unquestioning loyalty among his men. *National Archives*

Riding atop his captured British vehicle, a Dorchester armored car, Rommel traversed hundreds of miles of desert. The vehicle, dubbed by Rommel's staff as *Mammut* (mammoth) for its great size, was used as Rommel's command and communications center, his means of transport, and often even his sleeping quarters. It was inside this vehicle that Rommel found the British Perspex goggles that became his trademark the world over. Delighted when he found them, he said, "Booty permissible, I take it, even for a general." *National Archives*

The success of the resupply convoy was to be the *only* successful part of the operation. Careless radio transmissions by the British had tipped off Rommel's excellent intelligence gathering units. On June 14, 1941, the day before the Battleaxe was launched, a radio interception caught words likely to be code names to launch a major offensive. (Also, on the first day of battle, a listing of code words and call signs was captured.)

At 4 A.M. on June 15, Wavell's offensive began in earnest. It was designed as a three-pronged attack, in which the northernmost prong would slice along the coast, between the sea and the escarpment, to its objective of Sollum; the middle prong would wheel, parallel to the edge of the escarpment and south to Capuzzo and the Halfaya Pass; and the southern prong would circle around to attack Rommel's flank and rear. The hope was that Rommel would retire to Bardia, allowing British forces to open the way to Tobruk once again.

Wavell's plan was a disaster from the first day, due in large part to a new use for an old weapon. This battle

This light armored reconnaissance car packs a punch. It totes a 20-millimeter cannon and machine gun, like the larger Puma armored vehicles. *National Archives*

A German Panzerspahwagen Sd Kfz 234/1 Puma on the move. These eight-wheeled armored vehicles had a 20-millimeter cannon and 7.92-millimeter machine gun in an open-topped turret. All four axles were driven to help propel it through the sand without getting stuck, which often happened to two-wheel-drive cars and standard trucks. *National Archives*

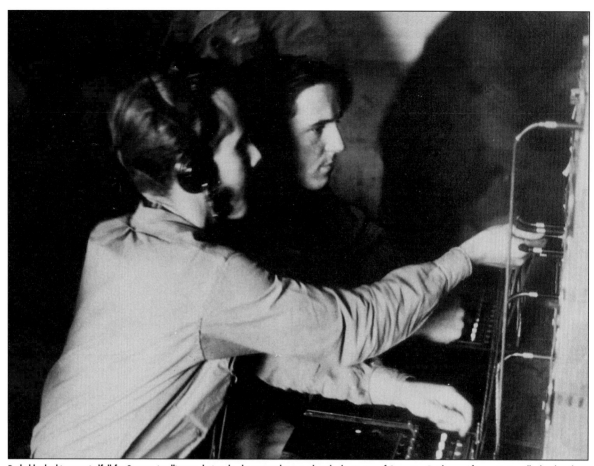

Probably the biggest windfall for German intelligence during the desert war happened at the beginning of Operation Battleaxe. After capturing Allied codes, the radio interception service deciphered British transmissions, which enabled them to plot British movement with precision and predict their plan of attack accurately. *National Archives*

saw one of the earliest uses of the German 88-millimeter antiaircraft gun as an antitank weapon. It was a simple idea that proved explosively innovative.

Rommel had only 13 of the guns, which he stationed at Hafid Ridge (7 miles west of Capuzzo) and Halfaya Pass. At both places, the Afrika Korps was well dug in and expecting the enemy's advance.

Dawn was just about to break when the Germans heard approaching tank motors. The troops at Halfaya were under the command of Captain Wilhelm Bach, a reserve officer who in civilian life was an Evangelical minister.

As Carrell wrote in *The Foxes of the Desert*, Bach stood beside an 88 calmly regarding the endless sand and still-distant enemy tanks. Dusk and dawn are very short transitions in the desert and, by now, the sun completely illuminated the battlefield, backlighting the squat silhouettes of tanks at about 3,500 yards. Bach ordered his men to hold their fire.

Suddenly there was a whistle of shells as the British tanks began firing. Explosive flashes and shell craters dotted the expanse before them. More British Mark IIs appeared over the horizon, followed by countless slower tanks and trucks bearing infantry troops. Closer and closer they came. When they reached the ruins of Halfaya village, the trucks stopped and the troops disembarked to proceed on foot alongside the tanks. The British still had no idea how close they were to the barrels of the German guns, which still sat silent.

Their advance now was "carefree . . . as if on a parade ground," Carell wrote. Then Pastor Bach gave the order and the full fury of the German guns broke loose. "Direct hits, columns of flame, more direct hits . . . the heavy turrets of reinforced steel were torn from the underhulls of the Mark IIs and flew several yards into the sand. A dozen burning tanks lay helpless in front of German positions. The 88-millimeter guns fired into the close-formation infantry columns, with murderous effect. From this moment, Halfaya was known as 'Hellfire' Pass."

Boxed 20-millimeter rounds await use in the cannons of armored cars. Getting supplies like this to the front-line troops was always a challenge in the trackless desert of North Africa. *National Archives*

Rounds are lined up alongside the barrel of a 20-millimeter cannon of a Panzerspahwagen Sd Kfz 234/1 Puma. *National Archives*

A 7.62-centimeter gun is ready and waiting for the British attack. *National Archives*

Originally designed as an antiaircraft gun, the 88-millimeter could propel flak shells 26,000 feet into the air. Rommel's units adapted it to the role of antitank weapon with deadly effectiveness. Here, spotters watch and report adjustments to the gun crew. At first, the 88-millimeter was used only in fixed positions, like this. Later, it was hauled on two-axled carriages behind half-track vehicles. It was an old weapon that, in its new use, would emerge as one of the most important weapons in desert warfare. In its earliest uses, the British tank crews thought they were under siege from a huge force of Axis armor when, in reality, few tanks met them head on, and the 88 fired at them from concealed positions on the flanks. *Rommelarchiv*

The German 88-millimeter gun crew consisted of a commander and an eight-man squad. The commander watched downrange to gauge accuracy. Based either on his own observation or from an observer alongside, he ordered the gunners to make lateral and elevation adjustments using traverse wheels. The crew could also adjust the fuse to explode at a set distance or on impact. When firing on tanks, only armor-piercing projectiles with fuses that exploded on impact were used.

The results, especially at Halfaya, were devastating to the British. The 88's deadly legacy is summarized in the official history of the North African campaign, published by Her Majesty's Stationery Office in 1956: "Operation Battleaxe, which had begun so hopefully, failed because Halfaya Pass could not be taken. The determination and firepower of the defense were too strong. The 88-millimeter guns, well concealed, proved deadly to any British tank. The surprise element also played an important role in the British defeat."

Simultaneously, the other two prongs of the British advance had engaged enemy positions. The center prong, the motorized infantry and tanks of the 4th Indian Division traversing the edge of the escarpment, fared better. They attacked Capuzzo, and by evening the town was in British hands once again. But the left-hand prong, the 7th Armored Division, received a reception at Hafid Ridge much like that at Halfaya Pass, with the wrath of the 88s raining down on them, too.

Despite heavy tank losses, the British pressed again on the second day. Rommel sent the 15th Panzer Division and the 5th Light Division, thus far kept in reserve, against what he thought were worn-down British armored units.

A shot from an 88-millimeter gun finds its mark in the distance. The guns could hit targets 2 miles away, but the gun crews usually waited until a tank approached within 1,000 yards, where the projectile could pierce even the thickest armor. *National Archives*

A British Matilda knocked out of commission, probably by 88-millimeter fire. *National Archives*

This British Matilda tank has a track off, but otherwise apparently is undamaged. It would probably be marked for recovery by Rommel's repair units. *National Archives*

German black crosses have been painted on the sides and front of this British Matilda tank. Because of their shortages the Germans in particular became quite adept at battlefield salvage and repair of Axis and Allied equipment. This tank could have fallen into German hands intact during the capture of one of the British strongholds, but more likely it was knocked out of action, recovered by German mechanics, and refurbished. Then it joined the ranks of a panzer division. The 30-ton Matilda had a top speed of 15 miles per hour, which made it slightly heavily and slower than its German equivalent. *National Archives*

**Germans scavenge
damaged equipment** *discarded by
the enemy. With the uncertainty of their
supplies, Axis units had to make do with
anything they could find. In reflex, they
developed a "pauper mentality," collecting all
sorts of battle-damaged equipment—guns,
tanks, and other vehicles—to refurbish them.*
National Archives

With smoke still pouring from their vehicles behind them, these British prisoners walk into captivity. Surrender was a last resort in a world war gone completely savage in other theaters. But capture by Rommel was far preferable to the SS death squads that executed prisoners on the European Continent. Rommel became known for his humane treatment of prisoners, with whom he shared rations of water, food and medical supplies equal to his own troops. *Rommelarchiv*

However, the 15th Panzer took a pounding. By the end of the second day, it had lost 50 of its 80 operational tanks. But its partner division to the west remained almost intact: The 5th Light crushed its brigade-strength opponent and advanced on toward Sidi Suleiman.

Rommel broke off the 15th Panzer's battle and directed it west to join the 5th Light. Unified, the two divisions overwhelmed any opposition that lay before them. On the third and final day, the British saw the futility not only in continuing with Battleaxe, but even in holding their ground. They cut their losses and pulled out.

Over the preceding weeks, Churchill had made thinly veiled threats about the consequences if Battleaxe failed. Wavell's dismal message back to London began with the simple statement of defeat: "I regret to report the failure of Battleaxe." Battleaxe was done, and so was Wavell. Within a week, Churchill replaced the great strategist who, with O'Connor just months before, had humiliated the larger Italian forces. In war, you're only as good as your last battle. Lieutenant General Sir Claude J. Auchinleck was appointed as Wavell's replacement.

North Africa was not the only sore spot now for Churchill. The British intervention in Greece, which had diluted the Western Desert Force, completely failed to halt the German invasion in late April. To top it off, many of the troops who escaped Greece had been evacuated to the island of Crete, and now that outpost was being threatened by a Nazi airborne invasion. British Empire troops were hurriedly removed to North Africa.

A lull of several months followed before another campaign began in North Africa. Hitler had ordered his army to invade Russia on June 22, 1941, and after that Rommel received no more reinforcements to press his advantage.

Rommel's victorious Cyrenaican campaign was soon known around the world. He was famous. He was ecstatic over victory. His star was rising toward its zenith.

Rommel looks on as Italian and German troops carry shovels to begin the work of digging in during the defense of Capuzzo and Halfaya. *National Archives*

German troops build gun emplacements on a hillside freshly abandoned by British forces. *National Archives*

Chapter Four

HARD FALL 1941

While in Cairo on August 8, 1941, an exasperated Winston Churchill had heard enough about Rommel. That's when he groused, "Rommel, Rommel, Rommel, Rommel! What else matters but beating him?"

That summer, Rommel's name was making headlines in *The Times* of London with an air of celebrity—unheard of for an enemy general. The focus of the British, and even the world was on the Desert Fox, but the Fox ignored what this flattering attention might bring—a renewed offensive against him in the fall.

Even as the British massed in Egypt to attack the Afrika Korps, Rommel chose to ignore the warning signs. His attention was elsewhere. As fall approached, he became increasingly obsessed with taking Tobruk. In enemy hands, it was a constant threat to his communication and supply lines; in Nazi possession, it would be an invaluable port to serve his own supply needs.

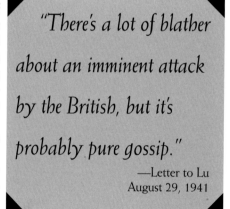

"There's a lot of blather about an imminent attack by the British, but it's probably pure gossip."

—Letter to Lu
August 29, 1941

But for him, the dream of taking Tobruk would turn into the nightmare of Britain's Operation Crusader in the fall of 1941.

Unending Supply Problems

Rommel *always* seemed to be operating at the end of a long, fragile supply line. Now it was true more than ever. His supplies had to travel some 300 miles from Benghazi or a brutal 900 miles from Tripoli, only to be disrupted within sight of German lines by raids launched from Tobruk.

Rommel was gifted in his ability to focus on an objective and formulate the combat tactics necessary to achieve it. But the same ferocious single-mindedness that made him a great tactician was also his downfall when it came to supplying his advance units.

The German leader concentrated so intently on tactical maneuver and the ultimate military objective that most anything else was taken as a distraction. He

Desert victories made Rommel a "media darling," drawing the attention of the entire world. He was followed by photographers and journalists wherever he went. This attention was largely due to Nazi Propaganda Minister Joseph Goebbels, who realized he had a propaganda gold mine in Rommel—young, skillful, patriotic, and representing the face of conquering Germany. *National Archives*

didn't regard the indispensable supply infrastructure in the same way the British did. Supply was not a pesky, peripheral nuisance to them. It was central to the British planning process to provide forward supply dumps, construct pipelines for fuel, extend railways or whatever else could be done to support the battle plan. They operated in the desert under the dictum, "Whatever you need you bring with you."

Speaking from the British point of view, Hacquebard deftly captured the direct tie between supply and the pattern of advance and retreat. In *Many Kinds of Courage* he wrote: "The 'Desert Fox' would push us one way, then we would push him back, until our supply lines got too long and became vulnerable. Then the Germans would bomb our supply lines and interrupt the flow of our petrol, water, food and ammunition, so that we would have to fall back again, shortening the distance between ourselves and our supplies, and stretching the distance the enemy's would have to travel. Then when Rommel's supply lines were vulnerable we would do the same thing to him."

Of course, Rommel also realized you had to bring whatever you needed in the desert. But he left it to the quartermaster to deal with the problem of building a plan for supply *around* his plan for battle.

An escort accompanies supply trucks 15 kilometers east of Tripoli. Even as they begin the journey eastward from the port city of their arrival, the threat of air attack is ever-present. This truck carries a potent passenger, a machine gunner with an AA gun at the ready to defend his supply convoy. *National Archives*

Rommel wrote, "The best thing is for the commander himself to have a clear picture of the real potentialities of his supply organization and to base his demands on his own estimate. This will force the supply staffs to develop their initiative and though they may grumble, they will as a result produce many times what they would have done if left to themselves."

His method of mapping out tactics and creating his battle plan first, while expecting that supply would simply respond to the demands placed on it, probably worked better on the European continent. In the barren and unforgiving desert, there was no "living off the land" to back up a shortfall in supplies. Indeed, the desert *was* a tactician's paradise and a quartermaster's hell—true especially for Rommel's quartermaster staff.

As the Afrika Korps chalked up victories that propelled it further and further east, lengthening the distance from the ports at Tripoli and Benghazi, even more care and attention needed to be devoted to the problem of supply.

On more than one occasion, his panzer divisions were brought to a standstill, stranded for lack of fuel—a highly vulnerable position for a tank to be in. With these cases, Rommel relied on luck; he gambled the British would not happen upon them and that supply trucks carrying gasoline would get through.

Greatly complicating the problem of supply was the fact that shipments to the Afrika Korps were sporadic, as a result of priorities for other operations, like

the invasion of Russia. Plus, the convoys faced a constant threat of attack from the RAF and Royal Navy. Responsibility for seaborne supply lay with the Italians, and with Rommel's already strained relations with Rome and his need for control, there was constant bickering and disagreement over supply issues.

In early August, when losses in shipping began to mount, it became clear that greater defenses in the form of aircraft and escort ships were needed. But Colonel General Franz Halder, now army chief of staff, would not support the request to strengthen Luftwaffe fighter cover to defend convoys traversing the Mediterranean en route to the African coast. Halder did, however, authorize cargo planes to bring in critical supplies, like 350 new tank engines that month.

To help overcome the problem of supply and to ease friction with the Italian Command, the German High Command intervened. Lieutenant-General Alfred Gauss was assigned as liaison with the Italian command in North Africa. However, instead of easing the friction, quite the opposite resulted.

Both Rommel and Gariboldi were irritated by Gauss's appointment, but for very different reasons. Gariboldi did not want another high-ranking German officer (and the large German staff that came with him) being injected directly into his headquarters. To him it was simply a transparent move to increase German influence in North Africa. It bothered Rommel because the high command dictated that Gauss would

With the Mediterranean Sea dominated by the Royal Navy for a time, Luftwaffe air transport becomes the only dependable means for critical deliveries to Africa. Between July and October 1941, 40 Italian ships were sent to the bottom. (These losses of equipment amounted to far more than what was lost in North African combat.) Supplies, once streaming into the bustling port at Tripoli, were reduced to a trickle. Meanwhile, tank engines, food, ammunition, and fuel had to be flown into desert airfields that summer. Here, a tri-engined Junkers 52 transport has just landed with supplies at Castel Benito, near Tripoli. *National Archives*

As the British grip on the Mediterranean tightened, safe arrival of supplies could not be taken for granted, as it had been in the first months after Rommel's arrival. Plus, Hitler gave priority of supplies to other Axis operations. Consequently, the Axis-controlled ports of Benghazi and Tripoli were sometimes quiet for weeks. In September 1941, Hitler gave his approval to send additional supplies for the Afrika Korps. One large shipment arriving at Benghazi thrilled Rommel enough to warrant specific mention to Frau Rommel in a letter dated September 29, 1941: "It took 50 hours to unload. You can imagine how pleased I was. With things as they are in the Mediterranean, it's not easy to get anything across. For the moment, we're only stepchildren and must make the best of it."

Rommel meets a new Italian officer under his command. As Rommel's forces were reinforced with additional Italian divisions, he had more subordinate Italian unit commanders. While he was extremely critical of his Italian superiors, he had praise for a number of Italian units serving under him. The different languages made for obvious communication problems, but Rommel spoke the language of command, which helped turn around the morale of the defeated Italian army in Africa. One of Rommel's first comments when he arrived in Tripoli was, "Most of the Italian officers had already packed their bags and were hoping for a quick return trip to Italy." That attitude changed as Italian units began to enjoy victories under Rommel's skillful direction. *Rommelarchiv*

Rommel meets with Gariboldi in the field. His relationship with the Italian high command was precarious at best. There were constant struggles over command decisions and supply responsibilities. *National Archives*

not fall within Rommel's chain of command. Gauss would act "independently."

A free-for-all ensued between Halder, Gariboldi, and Rommel. In the end, Rommel got his way, probably because of his personal influence with *Der Fuhrer*. Instead of Gauss operating independently from Rommel inside Gariboldi's command, Rommel declared in no unconditional terms that *all* of the Wehrmacht in Africa was under his command, and his command alone. In the end, Gauss would serve as Rommel's chief of staff.

Escalation and Reorganization

The Afrika Korps was strengthened and upgraded in name as the Panzergruppe Afrika (Panzer Group Africa) late that summer. It now included six Italian divisions and the Afrika Korps, consisting of three German divisions—the 15th and 21st Panzer Divisions and 90th Light Division (the 90th Light was a consoli-

dation of "miscellaneous" units already in North Africa and the 21st Panzer was the old 5th Light simply renamed). Troop strength from all these divisions numbered 55,000 men. There were 400 tanks, but only 250 were the formidable German designs.

British forces also were reorganized and stepped up in September. At about the same time the Afrika Korps became a sub-unit of the Panzergruppe Afrika, the Western Desert Force became the British Eighth Army. Auchinleck, as Middle East commander-in-chief, appointed a new commander for the Eighth Army: Major General Sir Alan Gordon Cunningham. Also strengthened, the Eighth Army was comprised of the 10th Corps, 13th Corps, and 30th Corps. It now had 200 Matilda tanks, 300 Cruiser tanks, 300 American Stuart light tanks, 600 field guns, 250 antiaircraft guns, 200 antitank guns, and 85,000 men. Much of the personnel could be traced back to the old Western Desert Force

As the Afrika Korps expanded into the Panzergruppe Afrika, there was an influx of supplies and more firepower. Here an 88 crew stands by its half-tracked prime mover ready to pull an 88-millimeter gun and a newly developed wheeled carriage laden with ammunition and supplies. *National Archives*

that was diverted to Greece in early 1941. These soldiers had come full circle, evacuated to Crete after defeat on the mainland, and now returned to North Africa. Now Auchinleck actually had more troops under his command than Wavell had the previous spring.

With the escalation of forces, Rommel now had acquired some strong-minded, battle-hardened commanders under him. Generals Ludwig Cruwell and Johannes von Ravenstein were independent operators, in the same fashion as Rommel himself. So with larger forces and strong-willed men in command of them, Rommel found himself a step further removed from field command.

Rommel Blunders

German raids on isolated posts continued to yield treasures like Dodge and Ford trucks (acquired by the British through U.S. lend-lease) and other equipment. The continuing success of these raids convinced Rommel that the British were demoralized and weak, and that Auchinleck was not prepared to go on the offensive.

In actuality, Auchinleck was ready to attack. He went to great lengths to hide his plans, but the influx of men and equipment into the British camp could not escape all eyes. Italian operatives reported tell-tale activity, but Rommel disregarded all intelligence reports that predicted an Allied offensive. Even photos of new supply depots that included vehicles and new airfields did not convince him.

Rommel did not want to be distracted from plans for his own offensive. Perhaps riding high on his recent spectacular victories or intoxicated with a feeling of invulnerability, he cavalierly planned the attack on Tobruk.

Plus, a more personal agenda had his attention. He was turning 50 on November 15, 1941, and he had planned for weeks to meet his wife in Rome to celebrate. On October 26, he handed down the plan for the Tobruk assault to his staff to begin the groundwork

Easy victories over remote outposts by small probing patrols, using weapons like this gun mounted on a small reconnaissance car, led Rommel to believe that British forces were weak. Quite the opposite was true. When the British launched their offensive, Rommel was taken completely by surprise. *National Archives*

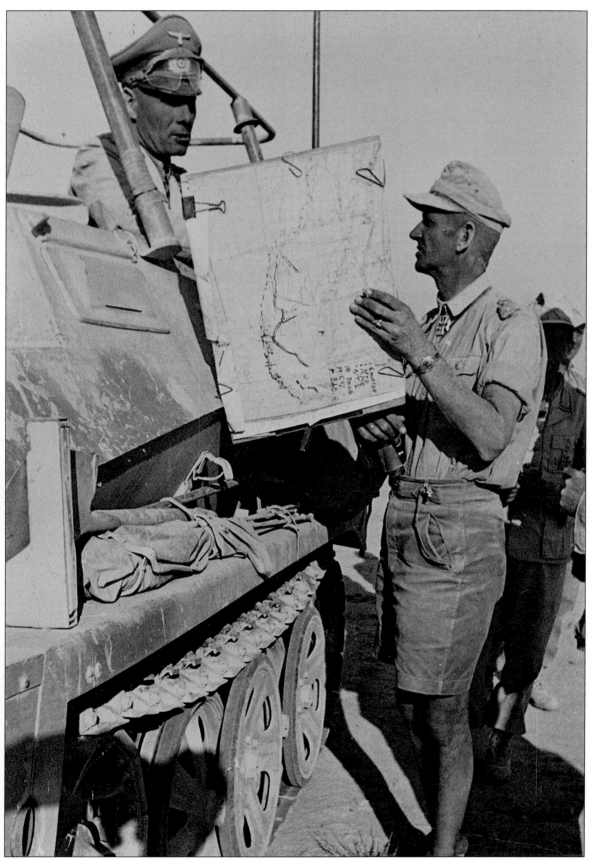

A profusion of German and Italian intelligence information is shown to Rommel just before the British launched Operation Crusader. Despite the hard evidence from a variety of sources, including reconnaissance reports and aerial photos, Rommel remained convinced that British forces were not ready for an offensive. *National Archives*

Field Marshal Sir Claude J. E. Auchinleck, the "Auk," writer of the memo that warned "Rommel is becoming a kind of magician or bogey-man to our troops…" With that, he had given a great albeit unwitting accolade that would fuel the Rommel legend. Auchinleck, formerly commander-in-chief in India, exchanged jobs with Wavell, after Wavell's counteroffensive (Operation Battleaxe) failed miserably. Auchinleck would be the mastermind behind Operation Crusader, which sent Rommel's forces reeling backward through Cyrenaica. *National Archives*

The British stand strong and ready for the masterstroke that would rid the desert of the Axis menace once and for all. For days, they impatiently awaited Rommel's "imminent" attack on Tobruk so they could spring their trap. Rommel, oblivious, was on holiday for most of the week, celebrating his 50th birthday with Frau Rommel in Italy. *National Archives*

while he was gone. Delegating loosely to Cruwell and von Ravenstein, he told them that the attack was to be launched November 20 and that he would return by November 18. Then he flew off to Rome.

While he was gone, the ominous news of a British buildup continued to mount. Prisoner interrogations supported the evidence of a coming offensive. Unmistakable armored and infantry columns were sighted approaching the frontier. Aerial photos showed clear images of newly extended railway lines and forward supply dumps.

Rommel's staff continued to carry out preparations for their own offensive as directed. They did no more to convince their hard-headed leader of the increasingly blatant evidence of a coming enemy offensive.

Tense Prelude to the Offensive

Auchinleck put the finishing touches on the plan to launch his first major offensive against Rommel. Code-named Operation Crusader, it called for a massing of armor in forward positions to overwhelm Rommel and send the Germans back across the desert. Auchinleck and Cunningham would send an infantry division toward Tobruk with the hope of luring the 15th and 21st Panzer Divisions out of their defensive positions in the Bardia area. Then the 30th Corps could move in to destroy them. Other British corps would line up toe-to-toe opposite Axis units near Capuzzo, Bardia, and Sidi Omar. They would tie them up and prevent them from coming to the aid of the panzer divisions.

It was a good, safe plan, but Auchinleck hesitated. Perceiving how important Tobruk was for Rommel's eastward advance, Auchinleck knew another German attack on the British-held port would occur soon. Further fueling Auchinleck's belief was a hand-drawn German map that fell into his hands. Incredibly, it showed a detailed plan for Rommel's attack, which called for an approach from the south and the east. To this day, it's not clear how the plan was betrayed or lost, and at the time, Auchinleck could not be sure of the map's accuracy. However, he was confident enough in its authenticity to delay his own offensive and draft a bolder plan.

As desert fighting becomes extremely confusing, units lose track of where they are and where other friendly units are. Here, there's evidently confusion in direction, as a command car meets a column of armored vehicles and tanks passing the opposite way. The officer from the car has gotten out to discuss direction and location of friendly units with the column leader. *National Archives*

A lull leaves Axis troops waiting as well. With Rommel's absence and Auchinleck's decision to await the Axis offensive, an uneasy quiet settled on the desert. This stationary 88-millimeter gun stands idle in a well-excavated position with a single crewman. Had Auchinleck launched his offensive, this gun would have presented a difficult target, being almost invisible in the shimmering landscape. Before it would have been spotted by approaching British tanks, the 88 crew likely would have delivered a devastating surprise. *National Archives*

Idle moments during Rommel's absence left the British checking and rechecking equipment while waiting for the enemy offensive. *National Archives*

It certainly beats trudging through the sand. Italian infantry troops ride atop a Panzer III. Following the initial assaults in Operation Crusader, Axis troops raced east as fast as their vehicles could, to try to overtake the fleeing British, in "the dash to the wire." *National Archives*

Instead of just pushing the Germans back out of Cyrenaica, Auchinleck saw an opportunity to decisively defeat the Axis in Africa once and for all. This required tremendous restraint and stealth—and all available forces left in Egypt. British moves could not be allowed to arouse suspicion that the German plan was known. Certainly no extraordinary attention was given to the southern and eastern defenses of Tobruk. Above all, Auchinleck ordered no conspicuous troop movements to tip off the massing of British forces from Egypt.

However, the secret movement of so massive a force was a huge challenge. It was imperative to move quickly across the desert sands under the cloak of darkness and strict radio silence. With a combination of skill and luck, it worked. No German reconnaissance patrols happened upon the great columns moving toward them. Luftwaffe reconnaissance pilots were duped as well.

German soldiers
literally dash to the wire—
barbed wire on the Egyptian
frontier. National Archives

Rommel helps free an MB 340 personnel carrier from sand. With his constant presence on the front lines, Rommel might be called a "hands-on manager" today. Rommel's practice of scouting the front lines for firsthand observation, often apart from his troops, presented more challenges than just getting stuck in the sand. He had numerous close brushes with the enemy or simply found himself separated from his command center at key junctures of battle, to the dismay of his subordinates. Joining in to push out the car, as well as eating the same food, sleeping in the same miserable conditions, and facing the same battlefield dangers as his men, assured that Rommel received the total devotion of his troops. *National Archives*

By November 14, 1941, the additional British forces were assembled and ready. They lay in wait, poised to watch as Rommel's forces formed into their offensive position just as expected. Then Auchinleck would spring the trap and attack where Rommel was most vulnerable, on his right flank.

But in the same way that the elusive Desert Fox had confounded his adversaries throughout the North African campaign, he didn't do what was expected. The attack didn't come.

The Eighth Army, chained like a great, snarling mastiff, was left to wait. With an understatement characteristic of the British, Auchinleck wrote in the foreword to Young's *Rommel the Desert Fox*, "Rommel gave me . . . many anxious moments."

November 14. November 15. November 16. All these days passed and, still no Rommel, no German attack.

By November 17, Churchill and his War Cabinet demanded action. For all they knew, Rommel had detected the British buildup and modified his plan. Or

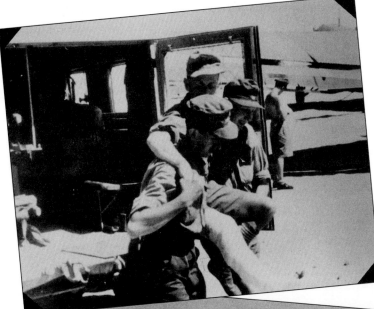

Casualties mount to staggering numbers

in Operation Crusader: 38,000 Germans killed, wounded or missing. Medics worked around the clock during each new assault. Ambulances shuttled the wounded to the rear, where sometimes the injured soldier received a ticket home. Here a wounded soldier is being lifted out of an ambulance for embarkation aboard an aircraft that will carry him home to Europe.

Not all wounded were immediately found. Stories about being wounded alone in the desert smack of old western movies. In Steinhoff's Voices from the Third Reich, a downed Stuka gunner, Gerhard Beck, described his experience of lying in the brutal sunshine with two bullet wounds near Tobruk on June 4, 1942: "I had shut my eyes, but was still awake when I felt something move against my right leg. I jerked my leg away and looked up. I saw a large vulture hopping backwards, wings flapping clumsily. There were two or three more behind him. Apparently, they had sat there a long time until the most daring of them had hopped up to see if I was in a proper state for consumption. Now he squatted about two steps away from me, dirty-white wings folded, bare neck stretched forward, crooked beak half open, staring at me with his black eyes: the picture of greed personified. By then I had figured out that I would probably die of thirst, but to be eaten by vultures was too much. I pulled out my pistol, which was rather difficult since I was lying on top of it. The vulture just stood there and stared at me the whole time without moving. I took a breath, aimed at the vulture, pulled the trigger, and instantly saw a red spot on the yellowish-brown feathers of its breast. It fell over, and I used the rest of my bullets on the other vultures. Except for one. I wanted to save one shot as a reserve." Beck lay for more than 24 hours, ravaged by direct sun and swarming flies before two German medics in a small Red Cross plane found and evacuated him.

Soldiers with minor wounds and desert afflictions line up outside an Arab house that has been converted into a doctor's office. Most field medical units set up hospital tents not far from front-line fighting. With the ebb and flow of desert battle, as units constantly advanced and retreated, the luxury of a permanent building like this at an oasis would not be enjoyed long.
National Archives

A German hospital ship lies at anchor in the Mediterranean awaiting the scores of wounded from each offensive. One German doctor serving under Rommel, Dr. Hans-Jurgen Brandt, recorded in *Voices from the Third Reich:* "We were always getting people fresh from the front, some in hopeless condition. As a doctor, you sometimes reached the point of despair." *Rommelarchiv*

the captured map, upon which Auchinleck had based the positioning of tens of thousands of men, could have been a fake.

Auchinleck remained steadfast. He held firm to his plan and sent replies to London stating that he would wait.

The response from Churchill was: "For the first time the troops of Great Britain and Empire are meeting the Germans with a profusion of weapons of all types. The result of the battle will influence the whole course of the war. It will be necessary to deal the heaviest blow for final victory, for our homeland and for freedom. The Desert Army will write a new page in history, comparable with Blenheim and Waterloo. The eyes of the world are upon you. All our hearts are with you. May God uphold the right." And the deadline to launch the offensive was dictated: the next day, November 18.

Assassination Attempt

During all of this high drama, the British paid Rommel the ultimate tribute to an enemy—assassination. Churchill termed it in his memoirs a "strike at the brain and nerve-center of the enemy's army at the critical moment." A commando squad was sent for the hit at Beda Littoria, far west of the front. From two sub-

marines, the squad paddled ashore in rubber boats under cover of night on November 17, 1941, within hours of Operation Crusader's launch.

Darting from shadow to shadow, they approached a grouping of houses commandeered by the Germans as a distant-rear headquarters. Based on British intelligence and tips from Arab collaborators, Rommel was living in one of the houses. Slipping past the lightly guarded perimeter, the commandos burst into "Rommel's house" with machine guns blazing. Four members of Rommel's quartermaster staff were instantly killed. The commandos were killed or eventually captured.

Rommel was oblivious to all of it. Oblivious to the fact that he was supposed to be attacking Tobruk, and that Churchill, Auchinleck, and 100,000 Tommies were impatiently waiting for him. Oblivious to the fact he was supposed to be in Beda Littoria for a rendezvous with the assassination squad.

He'd been quietly enjoying the last several days in Rome with his wife. The couple celebrated his 50th birthday by attending the opera on November 15 and touring the historic Roman ruins.

When he heard about the attempt on his life, he ordered that the captured commandos should be treated as regular POWs and not shot as spies, and that the British dead should be buried with full military honors alongside

Two German graves near Via Balbia: Fritz Braun and Otto Blasi, obscure soldiers identified among the fallen in the bloody first year. In the chaos of desert fighting, many soldiers were never identified and lie in nameless graves (as the two aligned behind). *National Archives*

Rommel visits one of many military cemeteries that lay in the wake of the fierce fighting. He stands rigidly, almost at attention, out of respect for the newly deceased soldiers. Note both graves have blankets draped over them; they soon will have a rock covering to shields the bodies from desert scavengers. *National Archives*

the four German soldiers who were killed. Then he dismissed it as an isolated, unfortunate incident and did not link it to a larger plan. He did not see it for what it was: an attempt to eliminate him at the critical moment when his forces would most need their strong leader.

Finally, Operation Crusader

On November 18, Rommel returned to Africa, to Gambut, where his new Panzergruppe Afrika was headquartered. Glancing out the aircraft window, he might have thought for a moment that the Junkers 88 flying him back had touched down on the wrong field, perhaps even on the wrong *continent*.

The sky was blotted over with solid black clouds. It was cold, and rain had been failing off and on since the night before. Torrential rivers had appeared, carrying away tents, equipment, bridges and even men. Shifting sands churned up by the moving water caused mines to explode and overturned trucks.

Amidst the confusion wrought by Mother Nature, he was met immediately with reports that the British had begun fanning out across the vast plain northwest of Fort Maddalena (on the Egyptian border) and that they were reconsolidating en masse at Gabr Saleh. And they were skirting the German flank south of Sidi Omar.

Perhaps it was the new structure of Panzergruppe Afrika that left him one step removed from the action. Perhaps it was his utter absorption with Tobruk. Or perhaps his mind was not yet focused on the matters at hand after his pleasant and peaceful leave. But for whatever reason, Rommel's fabled "sixth sense" that had repeatedly detected the approach of enemy troops failed him this time.

Even when General Cruwell said that *he* sensed an full-scale offensive, Rommel *still* did not believe this was a large-scale attack, a major offensive. Unbeknownst to him, the methods he himself had used so often and so successfully—stealth, lightning quick movement, and flank attack—now were being employed against him.

The rain had prevented even routine reconnaissance flights, so the Eighth Army enjoyed the benefit of total surprise right up to the launch. Luftwaffe pilots had been unable to confirm the vast numbers of men and tanks that were being positioned on the Egyptian frontier.

And Rommel, with the stubborn single-mindedness that had often served him well, still clung to his own plan to attack Tobruk. He did not want to be distracted from his offensive in reflex to "small" British moves.

Crusader began in earnest with a British three-pronged attack from the south. The prongs were elements of the Eighth Army's 30th Corps, under the command of Lieutenant General Willoughby Norrie. They

Rommel discusses alternatives with Oberstleutnant (lieutenant colonel) Bayerlein at his headquarters at Gambut, not far off the Via Balbia. Rommel's forces suffered severe losses in Operation Crusader, but he continued counterattacks, despite recommendations from his capable subordinates like Bayerlein. The counterattacks were weak and pointless, as Auchinleck was ready at every turn. The RAF and the Eighth Army's artillery struck at the aggressors—and German losses mounted further. *National Archives*

avoided Rommel's greater defenses of Sollum and Bardia. The east prong encountered the 21st Panzer Division, which inflicted great punishment on it. The middle prong surged past light defenses near Sidi Rezegh, on top of the escarpment about 10 miles from the sea coast and Tobruk. The west prong ran into resistance from the Italian Ariete Division. Simultaneously, the division at Tobruk launched an attack into the rear of the German lines, hoping to link up with Cunningham.

Now there was no denying that this was a full-scale offensive. Rommel tossed aside his plans for Tobruk.

Norrie shifted tanks from the west prong to shore up his forces in their battle against the 21st Panzer. The prongs began to blur across a 20-mile wide front as forces moved to support any advance as it occurred on Crusader's second day, November 19.

In response to this shift and some internal British entanglements, Rommel tried to focus his outnumbered forces on weaker elements of the 30th Corps. Rommel somehow became convinced that British tanks were closing in on Bardia, and he dispatched forces under General Cruwell to head off a fourth "prong," which turned out to be nothing.

In actuality, the British had turned their attention toward Sidi Rezegh. They concentrated their forces there when it looked hopeful that the 70th Division would break out of Tobruk and hook up with the

Rommel refuses to admit defeat

in early December 1941, even after the nearly complete annihilation of his forces. Here, an 88-millimeter antiaircraft gun opens fire on an approaching British tank near Sidi Rezegh. Although the counterattacks were largely ineffective, the deadly 88s did continue to find their marks. The result is a smoking British Matilda tank, out of commission.
National Archives

British units near Sidi Rezegh. But General Cunningham made a mistaken assumption that the British 4th Armored Brigade had overwhelmed Rommel's tanks. In reality, Rommel had decided to withdraw toward Sidi Rezegh as a defensive measure, when he deduced the British plan for a hookup with Tobruk.

Mass Confusion: Rommel Visits a British Hospital

The battle ensued around Sidi Rezegh in a melee that typified the confusion of desert fighting. As units pushed forward, odd situations developed that left both Axis and Allies in pockets vulnerable from all directions. As dusk turned quickly to the inky blackness of Crusader's first night, many men found themselves completely lost with no notion of where the enemy or friendly units were.

Rommel was among them. In his *Mammut*, he found himself weaving in and out of enemy columns. No one noticed because of the familiar silhouette cast by the captured British vehicle and the fact that it was too dark to see the black German crosses painted on its sides and back.

In fact, the confusion was so great that the next day Rommel was believed to have visited a *British* field hospital. It happened in the region near Sidi Rezegh. As Rommel neared a field hospital, he sent the main body on ahead while he decided to stop a few minutes for a morale-boosting stop.

Rommel and a few staff officers strolled casually into the compound of tents. He saw wounded German soldiers convalescing on cots. When he spoke words of comfort to them, the patients who recognized him must have been dumbfounded. The British doctors assumed this visitor in foreign uniform was a high-ranking Polish officer.

It's not known when Rommel realized his mistake, but he must have begun to suspect something when he heard British doctors and nurses in uniform talking in English as they milled about freely, conducting their mission of mercy for both British and German soldiers.

At some point, Rommel whispered to his aide, "It would be best to leave now." They eased out of the compound before being detected and disappeared over the dunes in a cloud of dust.

Surprising Moves

When the smoke cleared, Rommel's units, under the command of Cruwell and von Ravenstein, had won the day . . . or at least they had kept the British from winning. The Germans captured the airfield at Sidi Rezegh, but they suffered staggering losses. Smoldering tanks were strewn across the desert battlefield. Blackened hulks of exploded trucks, surrounded by bits and pieces of metal and flesh, were everywhere.

With the breakout of Tobruk still on his mind, Cunningham had ordered the 13th Corps, spearheaded by the New Zealand Division, to advance toward the port city's northern edge.

Rommel repulsed their first advance, but another one seemed more than his battered forces could endure. Rommel was faced with a decision. He could mass all his forces to crush the 13th Corps, but this could allow the 30th Corps to regroup and slash through to Tobruk at his rear. Or he could play it safe and follow the direction of his superior, Hitler, and pull back to Gazala until his forces were strengthened.

The Desert Fox surprised everyone. He chose *none* of the apparent options, and ignored Hitler's direction.

Instead, he drew together all his surviving tanks and set out to crush the 7th Armored Division. Despite the battered condition of his units, he set out to bulldoze southeast through the 7th Armored and continue to Sidi Omar, where he would attempt to attack the rear of the 13th Corps. This would allow a hookup with elements of the Afrika Korps still holding Bardia and Halfaya Pass.

The battle was confused and erratic already, but after Rommel's unexpected move, troops of both sides were baffled. Understanding of the battle and control of it quickly slipped from Cunningham's hands.

Cunningham couldn't ignore the fact that he had lost several hundred tanks. And he shrank at the thought of his vulnerable infantry divisions being crushed by the rampaging panzers. In the meantime, the security of the Egyptian frontier was at stake.

In desperation, he called for Auchinleck to come from Cairo. After Auchinleck reviewed the details of the situation, he saw no recourse but to "fight to the last tank." The original offensive would pound on, no matter how strong Rommel's will.

But the confusion Rommel created with his unexpected attack on the 7th Armored still left the British reeling. His plan was to skirt the flank of the 30th Corps and come upon them from behind, forcing them to fall back into the minefields he had set up near Sollum and Halfaya. The plan was good and might have worked, had he followed through with it.

But Rommel, too, became overanxious or perhaps confused in the chaos that he himself had created. Operating from the head of his panzer column, he gave the order to move out before the majority of his forces were ready. Intolerant of the pesky housekeeping of supply, he did not even wait for all his panzers to be refueled.

The Dash to the Wire

Rommel set out at midmorning on November 24 with only one panzer regiment. Fuel trucks had arrived to fuel the rest, but that would take until noon. Rommel set his sites on the Sollum front and plunged forward.

Rommel rode in the lead tank in this impromptu surge into the complete unknown. Bayerlein said it was a "wild drive" and "in complete disregard of the British threat to their flanks."

Even though Rommel's force was not large or strong, it caused utter panic among the British rear echelons. Supply units and staff officers, unaccustomed to the melee of a wide-open desert tank battle, were caught completely by surprise.

In sheer panic, they retreated for nine hours to get back to what was called "the wire"—the Egyptian border. Although the Germans were only seen as plumes of rising dust on the horizon, everyone was withdrawing as if the might of the entire Wehrmacht were bearing down on them.

General Cunningham panicked as well, which probably sealed his own fate as commander of the Eighth Army. As shelling began to rain down on the airfield, Cunningham narrowly escaped in a Blenheim aircraft and made it through to his headquarters at Maddalena. Awaiting him there, Auchinleck made the decision to relieve him. Cunningham's replacement was Lieutenant General Neil Ritchie.

Rommel pushed on and "crossed the wire" by late afternoon, with the rest of his forces stretched out in a staccato column 40 miles behind him. Then he went another 20 miles and wheeled around northward to hook up with German units at Halfaya Pass and Sidi Omar, as he'd hoped.

Accompanied by General Gauss, he left the head of the column to retrace his steps backward to the border. However, Rommel's lone vehicle, in the middle of the desert, broke down. Again, incredible luck was with him. As Gauss and Rommel stood at the border, awaiting a fate they could not know, the silhouette of a *Mammut* poked above the rise of a distant dune. Black crosses identified it as one of his own. With the casualness of a taxi cab pulling over to pick up a patron on the curb, General Cruwell's *Mammut* stopped to pick up his German colleagues.

Cruwell was lost also. While the battle reignited in the distance, Rommel and his generals were meandering in the dark through British territory without any notion of where friendly or enemy units were, or where they were. In the meantime, Panzergruppe Afrika continued fighting without its top two levels of leadership. In their absence, Colonel Westphal assumed command.

When Rommel finally appeared among his own units, the battle was out of control. Auchinleck was better able to keep his forces organized and he still re- solved not to back down. Auchinleck turned out to be a match for Rommel's will and tactical genius. Initially, Rommel was enraged with Westphal's decisions that had deviated from his plan, but he eventually realized it was not Westphal's fault.

At first, the Germans were almost amused by the stampede they'd caused, then they realized the vulnerable state they were in. They were now besieged on all sides by enemy attacks as a result of the hasty decision to plunge east with little regard as to how to consolidate their gains. To make matters worse, they'd left the German holding force near Sidi Rezegh vulnerable. Elements of the 30th Corps had not retreated and were punching toward Tobruk. In the process, they recaptured the Sidi Rezegh airfield.

Rommel returned west, all the while being pummeled by flank attacks, to launch a counterattack at Sidi Rezegh that lasted three days. The 2nd New Zealand Division (part of the 30th Corps) fought tenaciously.

By November 27, Rommel began to regain control when his two panzer divisions were able to hook up. These forces were strong enough, for a time, to keep the New Zealand Division at bay and prevent a British advance toward Tobruk. But one by one, he was losing tanks, until nearly all of Panzergruppe Afrika had been destroyed in this costly "dash to the wire."

On November 29, the New Zealanders captured the 21st Panzer Division commander, von Ravenstein, along with his maps. Even with the handicap of this loss and compromised plans, Rommel was able to surround the New Zealanders and capture nearly 1,000 of them.

Rommel later wrote in summary: "Rivers of blood were poured out over miserable strips of land which, in normal time, not even the poorest Arab would have bothered his head over."

British reinforcements were now streaming toward the area and Rommel's forces had no reserves left to call in. In *Panzer Battles*, Major Freiherr von Mellenthin summed it up this way: "On paper, we (the Afrika Korps) seemed to have won the Crusader battle, but the price paid was too heavy. The Panzergruppe had been worn down, and it soon became clear that only one course remained—a general retreat from Cyrenaica."

After Rommel's divisions regrouped, the devastation was clear. There had been a great price paid in human life. For the Germans, there were 38,000 men killed, wounded or missing; for the British, nearly 18,000. Tank losses numbered about 300 for the Germans and at least that many for the British, but pinpointing a precise number is difficult due to the gradually improving technique for recovery and repair of battle-damaged tanks. Of course, tank losses did not hurt the British nearly as much as the supply-starved Germans.

**Driven back
across Cyrenaica,**
*the Germans set up their
camps, sometimes
in precisely the same locations
they'd occupied the previous
spring. This bunker
is complete with walls and
"cupboards."*
National Archives

Rommel refused to admit defeat. Even with the losses staring him in the face, he went on with a series of bloody and mostly ineffective counterattacks. His usual superb instincts and good judgment on the battlefield had diminished after weeks of constant battle. His commanding generals carried out orders, but they clearly did not believe in the cause. Retreat from Cyrenaica was the only reasonable option remaining for the Afrika Korps.

On December 3, Rommel sent forward a ragtag force to the positions he was forced to leave stranded at Sollum, Bardia and Halfaya Pass. The attempt to hook up with and evacuate these outposts failed, as the RAF strafed and artillery shells pounded the rescuers. On December 4, he launched another pointless counterattack against Auchinleck just east of Tobruk. It was repulsed.

On December 5, he made one last surge at El Gubi, which was entirely anticipated by Auchinleck. Again the Germans were repulsed, but only after heavy casualties and the loss of more precious tanks. By this date, Rommel's units had been chopped to 10 percent of their original complement. In the ebb and flow of desert fighting, Rommel retook Bardia and Gambut, but the British were able to break through to Tobruk on December 11. Rommel ended up being the one who fought, in Auchinleck's words, "to the last tank." This was the German general's first major defeat.

It was clear that if only he'd shown restraint before plunging headlong in the "dash to the wire," the Germans might just have withstood Crusader—maybe even won. But the result of the quick thrust through the desert was defeat. And this wasn't the only devastating news for Rommel.

On the other side of world, sudden aggression had "awakened the sleeping giant." The Imperial Japanese Navy had bombed Pearl Harbor, Hawaii, on December 7. The United States entered the war and mobilized its population and industry toward the singular goal of crushing the Axis forces. Almost immediately after America's entry into in the war, Churchill and President Franklin Roosevelt agreed that the defeat of Germany should be the top Allied priority. The first step toward that goal was called Operation Super Gymnast—the invasion of North Africa. Already in the works, the Allied landings would be under the command of Lieutenant General Dwight David Eisenhower.

German Withdrawal through Cyrenaica

Cruwell accepted the fact that Panzergruppe Afrika had been weakened so badly that it must pull back, stop any attempts at counterattack, and abandon any thought of an offensive. He pleaded with Rommel to see the reality of the situation (an ironic prelude to a similar plea, when Rommel pleaded to Hitler for withdrawal from Africa altogether). But the desert saga was not yet over and there were still some victories remaining for Rommel.

Eventually, he accepted Cruwell's sound advice, and the remnants of his once-strong forces fell back to a position around Gazala.

While at Gazala, Panzergruppe Afrika was again attacked by British forces, now commanded by General Ritchie. Ritchie maneuvered to approach from the south, but the assault failed.

Still, Rommel concluded that he could not hold this position if all of the remaining British armor were massed against him. The decision was to march backward a humiliating 150 miles to Beda Fomm. This retreat meant abandoning the German troops holding isolated positions on the frontier at Sollum, Bardia and Halfaya Pass. This last unit included the now-legendary Wilhelm Bach, who had earned a field promotion to major. "Hellfire" Pass held on past Christmas against a South African unit of the Eighth Army.

As they clung to their positions, there was no holiday that year except " . . . words read to us from the Bible by Father Bach, our major and chaplain," a soldier recounted to Carrell in the *Foxes of the Desert*. "The Christmas bells were replaced by the British 25-pounder shells, which thundered down on our foxholes in the rocks. What a Christmas Eve!"

Benghazi was left to fall into British hands on Christmas Day, but Rommel was able to make one last good use of its port. An Italian vessel unloaded 22 precious new tanks there. Within a few days of their arrival on December 24, these tanks were baptized into battle. They joined remnants of the 15th Panzer that, in total, outnumbered the British 22nd Armored Brigade. The 22nd was surrounded and lost between 60 and 90 tanks in actions on December 28 and 30. The 22nd had no choice but to surrender. The battle took place near El Haseiat, which ended up being the furthest point of Britain's westward advance.

Auchinleck did not completely defeat Rommel, as he had hoped. Despite his mistakes, Rommel had been spared that. But over a period of six weeks, his forces were driven backward across 200 hard-won miles of desert to Benghazi, and then another 200 miles down the coast to El Agheila. His forces were a shadow of what they had been, and the British once again occupied most of Cyrenaica. At the end of 1941, Rommel was back where he had begun the previous spring.

Chapter Five

LIGHTNING TURNAROUND

The Afrika Korps received Christmas gifts from *Der Fuhrer*: an enormous influx of supplies. On December 23, 1941, a convoy bearing 23 tanks arrived in North Africa. On January 2, 1942, ships ferried 2,000 tons of gasoline for Rommel's thirsty panzer divisions. On January 5, the biggest shipment of all arrived: 54 more tanks, 20 armored cars, dozens of 88-millimeter guns, ammunition, food, and medical supplies.

These were among the many convoys that arrived intact that winter at the deep-water port of Tripoli. The bounty was due to German victories elsewhere. While Rommel's forces had been taking a pounding at the hands of the Eighth Army in November and December, the German Reichsmarine and Luftwaffe were successfully challenging British control of the Mediterranean.

The potent U-boats helped swing the balance of control to Germany. U-boat crews that had devastated Atlantic shipping were now unleashed in the

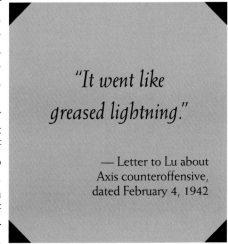

"It went like greased lightning."

— Letter to Lu about Axis counteroffensive, dated February 4, 1942

Mediterranean. As Admiral Karl Doenitz, commander-in-chief of the Reichsmarine, wrote in his memoirs, "The advent of these experienced crews had an immediate effect."

U-boats torpedoed the aircraft carrier *Ark Royal* and the battleship *Barham* in November, and the cruiser *Galatea* in December. All three British ships were sunk, along with the cruiser *Neptune* and destroyer *Kandahar* in a minefield near Tripoli in December. On the same day that *Neptune* and *Kandahar* were sent to the bottom, Italian midget submarines infiltrated Alexandria harbor and seriously damaged the battleship *Valiant* and the *Queen Elizabeth*.

RAF patrols that had ravaged the Axis shipping routes at will for months were chased off by reinforced Luftwaffe squadrons based in southern Italy. "The heavy Axis air raids against Malta, in particular, were instrumental in practically neutralizing, for a time, the threat to our sea routes," Rommel wrote. "It was this fact which made possible an increased flow of

A welcome sight for Rommel: A U-boat patrols the waters off the coast of Bardia. The U-boat presence helped win back control of the Mediterranean Sea. They not only transformed the hunters—Royal Navy warships—into the hunted, but they targeted British transports as well. *National Archives*

To Rommel, the influx of supplies at the end of 1941 translated into just one thing: resuming the offensive. Fuel, like that being wheeled in a barrel by a black laborer, is the lifeblood of a mobile army. Rommel didn't delay in putting it to use. *National Archives*

materiel to Tripoli, Benghazi and Derna—the reinforcement and refitting of the German-Italian forces thereupon proceeded with all speed."

With greater priority being given to Africa and the Mediterranean by the German High Command, the picture looked bright for continued resupply of the Panzergruppe Afrika. And while Rommel's strength was growing, Auchinleck's was diminishing. It was almost a replay of the year previous when the British "snatched defeat from the jaws of victory." British troops were diverted away from North Africa. Instead of moving into Greece, this time British forces were sent to meet the new challenge of halting the Japanese advance in the Pacific, particularly at New Guinea and Burma.

The classic Rommel response to this reversal of fortune was, "We'll take the offensive again!"

Preparations for the Perennial Offensive

British positions just east of El Agheila drew the attention of Rommel's staff. Intelligence reports suggested that these "strongholds" were weak. On January 12, Major von Mellenthin explained to Rommel that the window of opportunity for an attack would last only a couple of weeks, and after that the region would likely be reinforced. If they acted now, they had the rare advantage of superior numbers.

On the deck of a newly arrived U-boat, Rommel is grateful to the crew that surrounds him and delighted with the supplies they shepherded to port. *National Archives*

Destined for Rommel's forces in Africa, equipment is transported typically by rail from Germany through annexed Austria into Italy. There it would be loaded on ships at the ports of Genoa, Naples or Taranto and ferried across the Mediterranean Sea to the receiving ports of Tripoli, Tunis, Benghazi, Tobruk, or Mersa Matruh.

Rommel's forces
*had been subsisting on
a fraction of the supplies
they needed. Supplies
delivered early January
1942 satisfy the bare
necessities of both man
and machine: Ingredients
are quickly turned
into bread.*

*And the essentials for a mobile force,
including fuel and tires, are immediately dispersed.
The wartime caption for the bottom photograph, translated from
German, exhibits more than a hint of propaganda: "In the North
African Theater of War . . . a large supply of tires is always on
hand for the brave German soldiers, even on African soil."*
National Archives

With a priority for supplies now given to Rommel, the transport routes out of Tripoli are active again, getting much needed fuel, food, water, and ammunition to the front. *National Archives*

Rommel meets with Italian Army Chief of Staff Ugo Cavallero (center, with visor cap) and General Ettore Bastico, who had replaced Gariboldi. They arrived from Rome to accompany Field Marshal Kesselring in Libya during the last week of January 1942. Both Italian officers wear the Iron Cross awarded to them by the Germans. *National Archives*

At first, Rommel hesitated. But the intelligence reports convinced him. January 21 was set as the date of the counterstrike. Stung previously by indiscreet leaks in the chain of command (presumably on the Italian side) Rommel took unusual measures to maintain secrecy before the offensive. He explained in his log: "I had maintained secrecy over the Panzergruppe's forthcoming attack eastward from Mersa el Brega and *informed neither the Italian nor the German High Command.* We knew from experience that Italian Headquarters cannot keep things to themselves and that everything they wireless to Rome gets round to British ears."

All of the other usual ruses and precautions preceded the strike. Transportation of supplies was limited to nighttime only. Tanks were disguised as trucks with canvas and wood. Only critical reconnaissance was allowed. The night before the attack, parts of the village at Mersa el Brega and a ship in the harbor were set ablaze as if supplies were being destroyed before withdrawal.

The Second Cyrenaican Offensive

The plan was textbook perfect, and it was executed with precision. Rommel's reconstituted forces, now with the elevated title of Panzerarmee Afrika, launched

Sorting the daily mail:

When a supply convoy gets through, that means the mail does, too. Crucial for troop morale, mail reminds them that they are more than soldiers, but have hometowns and families worth fighting for. Mail sacks here show a few of those hometowns: Koblenz, Mannheim (home to Pastor Bach of Halfaya Pass), Stuttgart, and Frankfurt.

National Archives

an assault in a northeasterly direction toward Agedabia and Beda Fomm.

Everything seemed to work in Rommel's favor. Even the weather aided him, with a timeliness that had worked for the Eighth Army before Crusader. Sandstorms cloaked the advance of German tanks, and the sudden fury of a rainstorm began to flood the British airfield at Antelat. Just when air support was needed most, four RAF fighter squadrons were evacuated from Antelat to Msus, and one squadron was sent to Gazala.

By the morning of January 22, Rommel had taken Agedabia and Beda Fomm. On the afternoon of January 23, Ritchie returned from Cairo and casually underestimated the magnitude of the attack. As Rommel ignored clues about his enemy's actions at the beginning of Operation Crusader, Ritchie mistook the German offensive for "a reconnaissance in force."

The same day, Field Marshal Kesselring visited Rommel, with high-ranking Italians in tow. The Italian Army's chief of staff, Field Marshal Ugo Cavallero, and Gariboldi's replacement, General Ettore Bastico, came with orders direct from Mussolini to remain in a defensive posture. Six weeks before, Cavallero had tried to prevent Rommel from retreating past Gazala during Operation Crusader. Now, Rommel was told to stop an offensive, even though he "sensed" sure victory.

Cavallero stated in unmistakable terms that this was to be a raid, and nothing more. Rommel locked horns with his nominal superior and said that a full-fledged offensive would go forward and no one but *Der Fuhrer* could direct him otherwise.

Kesselring, in the unenviable position of intermediary, saw no point in supporting the Italians or arguing with Rommel. He left with Bastico and Cavallero grousing and Rommel reveling in his offensive.

By January 29, Rommel pushed up the coast through Benghazi, a significant port. There, newly delivered British supplies fell into his hands: Food, fuel and 1,300 trucks.

A few days later, Rommel wrote ecstatically to Frau Rommel about the offensive: "It went like greased lightning." Once again, he had made an astonishing turnaround from full retreat to advancing with great momentum.

Supplies mean rejuvenated forces and the equipment needed for an offensive: Half-tracks are loaded and ready for the order to move out. Rommel stands in the rightmost vehicle. *Rommelarchiv*

Rommel races along the front lines in his *Schutzen Panzerwagen,* or SdKfz250 le Sch PzWg. *Bundesarchiv*

A Nazi flag is used as a signaling device. From the turret of this Sd Kfz 234, the driver signals to troops in forward positions on April 9, 1942, somewhere in eastern Cyrenaica. *National Archives*

This greatly contrasted with his performance during Operation Crusader, when he had been sluggish, confused, even momentarily crazed. That defeat had sapped his colossal self-confidence. But showing the heart of a leader, he bounced back. Now, with his forces collected and mind focused, Rommel resumed the passion, discipline, quick thinking, and confidence he displayed in the spring of 1941 during his first Cyrenaican offensive.

In just two weeks, Rommel had bulldozed to the east, halfway across Cyrenaica. By February 6, the British had retreated beyond the coastal towns of Cyrene and Derna, all the way to Gazala. And in the process, British losses numbered 40 tanks and more than 1,400 troops. Rommel's losses were small.

For his success, Hitler promoted him to colonel general.

A Lull

While the British licked fresh wounds at Gazala, and the bulk of the Panzerarmee securely massed around Antelat and Mersa el Brega, all major action stopped. The lull continued until spring 1942.

At a camp *40 kilometers south of Derna, Rommel meets with General Ludwig Cruwell. Rommel is jovial over the recent capture of Benghazi, thanks in part to Cruwell's own superb execution of Rommel's plan.* National Archives

After small skirmishes over worthless, featureless terrain, a defensive front gradually evolved southward from Gazala. Called the Gazala Line, it was 60 miles of mobile and stationary defenses, girded by minefields. The British built six self-contained fortresses, descriptively called "boxes," along the Gazala Line. Each was 1 to 2 miles square. A couple of them, like Bir Hacheim, were built at existing settlements and kept their Arabic titles. The others were constructed on a barren plot of desert. The perimeter of each "box" was heavily mined and bristling

A Moslem temple near Derna is bypassed during the trek across the desert. Few buildings existed in the desert, and they had little or no tactical value, so most survived intact. Rommel issued specific orders not to harass the Arabs, and the sanctity of a temple would have been particularly off limits. Most of the natives were entirely impartial to Allies and Axis forces, so harassment of them had no military value and might only prompt vengeful sabotage. National Archives

The watchful eyes of a sentry scan the earth's broadest horizon at a lonely outpost, outside a reconnaissance battalion camp near Derna, Cyrenaica, on April 1, 1942. At first hint of an enemy ground or air raid, the sentry would stand, crank the warning siren, and run for camp. The siren had been captured from the British. (April 1, also in Germany, is April Fool's Day, but a prankish turn of the siren even on this day would likely not have been met with good humor.) National Archives

Victory shows on the faces of Rommel's infantry soldiers after they've charged most of the way across Cyrenaica. The next action they'll see will be at the Gazala Line, where the infantry is key to overcoming the "box" defenses. *National Archives*

with barbed wire and guns with measured fields of fire. At the center were enough supplies to last a week.

Roving between theses defensive positions were the Eighth Army's tanks. They patrolled hundreds of square miles south of Gazala looking for any German armor attempting to penetrate the line. Plus, if a "box" were attacked, the tanks would rush to its defense.

While Rommel was planning an attack on the Gazala Line, the question of Malta was still pending. Hitler was ready to commit resources to an invasion of the island. That would have been a big boost to the safety of Axis shipping in the long run, but it meant short-term diversion of resources away from Africa.

Rommel knew how important capturing Malta was to the larger hopes of Axis success in the Mediterranean. More than anyone, he wanted safe passage for Axis supply convoys across the Mediterranean, but Rommel questioned the timing and priority of a Malta invasion. Kesselring planned it in detail on paper, with

dates and units. But in the midst of a successful offensive, Rommel used his personal influence with Hitler to keep Africa as the priority.

Hitler directed that the drive into Egypt would take priority over invasion of Malta. This was the scenario within which Rommel's forces launched an attack on the Gazala Line.

Gazala Offensive

At a meeting in April, Hitler and Mussolini authorized Rommel to launch another offensive. But there was a condition—one that had to be dictated in no uncertain terms for the aggressive German general: Once Tobruk was captured, he was to assume a defensive position. Then, finally, Axis resources diverted from Africa would be brought to bear on Malta.

On the eastern side of the Gazala line, Auchinleck and Ritchie were planning an offensive of their own. Their preparations were characterized by the usual

British thoroughness. Supply dumps sprang up all along the front (with particular concentrations at Tobruk and Belhamed) containing thousands of tons of ammunition, medical supplies and food, along with millions of gallons of fuel.

When Rommel attacked first, in late May, these large supply dumps became tremendous liabilities for their British owners. In a free-wheeling armored battle, especially one with the twists and turns characteristic of Rommel, the need to protect a fixed point was like swimming with a stone around your neck. British maneuver was limited, because the supply dumps had to be protected.

On May 26, Rommel began with a diversion on the northern end of the Gazala Line, between the Mediterranean and Capuzzo. He traveled with the Afrika Korps, now commanded by General Walther Nehring. The Italian Ariete and Trieste Divisions followed. Rommel had two options: To muscle directly through the line or skirt around Bir Hacheim before breaking through.

The plan Rommel chose was to move south around Bir Hacheim, where there was a defensive "box"

A commander draws together his AA crew for a briefing in eastern Cyrenaica. While the RAF had been weakened for the time being in the area, the whine of the warning siren could have sent them into action at any moment. *National Archives*

at a bend in the Gazala Line. He expected to take Bir Hacheim in an hour, break through the line, then pivot north toward Acroma to smash British defenses from the rear. Within four days, he hoped to fight his way up the line, swallowing one "box" at a time, and seize the great prize of Tobruk.

The plan was wildly optimistic. With his 10,000 vehicles, Rommel was able to turn the corner around the south flank of Bir Hacheim, but not until early morning on May 27. Bir Hacheim refused to fall, so he issued orders for the Ariete Division to stay behind and take it. The order, however, never reached Ariete, so they continued their forward movement behind the German troops.

Rommel's men smashed forward, pounding the British 30th Corps. But that afternoon, he hit a wall of steel—new, American-made Grant tanks, with deadly 75-millimeter guns capable of blasting through the armor of German tanks. By that night, he had lost one-third of his armor.

General Fritz Bayerlein, Rommel's chief of staff, commented in Desmond Young's *Rommel, the Desert Fox*, "General Ritchie's dispositions were excellent. The

Even in the midst of pending battle, an occasional haircut is necessary. Hygiene in general was a problem, because of lack of water and even the most basic amenities. Hair in particular had its problems; on hair, the powdery sand, combined with sweat, turned into paste. *National Archives*

Rommel observes soldiers around their truck-mounted gun. Rommel was known for his watchfulness over the smallest details and his uncanny (and perhaps annoying) knack of immediately identifying any kind of tactical weakness. And, as his troops knew well, he was quick to speak up about it. *National Archives*

Great stores of fuel and ammunition in the desert are worth gold. But during the Gazala Offensive, the great supply dumps became a tremendous liability to the British, who had to plan their maneuvers based on protection of them. Rommel's complete mobility and freedom from defending any particular fixed geographic point helped him outmaneuver his adversary once again. *National Archives*

The most natural refrigeration: Italian soldiers dig a small pit where they will store water cans in the relative coolness of the earth to maintain its freshness. *National Archives*

American 'General Grant' tanks, too, with their 75-millimeter guns, came as a great surprise to us and 15th Panzer Division lost 100 tanks the first day."

Savage resistance brought the Germans to a dead stop midway between Bir Hacheim and the sea. This was just south of another box, which the British had called Knightsbridge Box. Breaking this position required assaults from the rear and front.

As usual Rommel was in the thick of it. In a letter to Frau Rommel, he wrote, "A shell splinter came through the window recently and landed in my stomach after going through my overcoat and jacket. All it left was a multicolored bruise the size of a plate. It was finally stopped by my trousers. The luck of the devil." It was true: An air of luck clung about him. Rommel's men noticed it too, and word spread about his imperviousness to personal harm.

Knightsbridge would not break and Rommel found himself bogged down. Plus, the 90th Light Division somehow had been separated from the main German front and British armor was taking advantage of the separation by pounding into it like a wedge.

Rommel's forces needed to regroup, so he backed them off to form a protective semicircle. With so many vehicles, it covered a vast area of perhaps 100 square miles, which came to be called "The Cauldron." All around it was a seething, lethal combination of minefields and British guns based in the box strongholds.

Rommel saw that his plan to crush the British forces behind the Gazala Line had not succeeded. He admitted that he had underestimated the strength of the British armored divisions. He looked for a way out.

Italian engineers intrepidly cleared a way through the minefields, but British artillery soon zeroed in on the passage.

Ritchie saw his chance to catch Rommel immobile, vulnerable, and growing short on supplies. From Cairo, Auchinleck ordered an attack immediately. But instead of massing his forces and waging an all-out attack, Ritchie threw in the armor in piecemeal "penny packets." Rommel took full advantage of this, engaging them as they advanced, to be picked off one by one.

When soldiers
aren't on the offensive *and trying to advance, they*
improve their own personal defenses in any way they can. Here, a trench is improved with walls of sand-filled British ammunition boxes. Camouflage is added to tents. National Archives

Eighty kilometers west of Bir Hacheim, Rommel meets with staff officers to discuss strategy on April 25, 1942. Near Bir Hacheim, Rommel would capture a Jewish brigade and order treatment for its soldiers equal to other POWs. This meant rations and medical treatment equal to that which his own men received—diametrically opposed to Nazi doctrine. *National Archives*

Two soldiers take a moment to look at the crumbling walls of the old fort at Capuzzo, where Italian and German flags fly again after its recapture. It's no wonder its walls are crumbling. In the see-saw battles of 1941 and 1942, occupation of the fort is known to have gone back and forth between the Axis and Allies *no less than five times.* *Rommelarchiv*

Tanks, half-tracks, trucks, and artillery, probably of the 90th Panzer Division, press on to the coastal town of Bardia. Terrain is such that vehicles can drive many abreast on firm ground. The approach to Bardia was actually a ruse; just as the British became convinced the column had its sites set on Bardia (where the British were on full alert for a division-strength assault), Rommel suddenly turned his column left and bore down on Tobruk. That night, as Rommel directed his units into position in the old familiar territory just south of Tobruk (where they had tried before to seize it and failed), they found undisturbed supply dumps just where they'd left them the previous April, with even more artillery shells with which to pound Tobruk. *Rommelarchiv*

Sappers, men with the delicate job of detecting mines, attempt to clear a safe path for the column that follows them. They would plant black flags behind them to mark that safe path. The Cauldron was made even more treacherous by the multitude of mines. *National Archives*

General Fritz Bayerlein, chief of staff of the Afrika Korps and later chief of staff of Panzergruppe Afrika. (Pictured here as a lieutenant colonel in December 1941.) Of all German officers excluding Rommel himself, Bayerlein saw more action in North Africa than any other. After serving with General Heinz Guderian's panzer army in Russia, Bayerlein arrived in Africa in October 1941. During the following 19 months, he was in the midst of grueling, continuous fighting. His service in Africa ended in May 1943, when he was wounded and evacuated just before the end. *National Archives*

On May 28, 1942, Rommel made the bold decision to forge ahead northward. Ritchie was not ready for the movement, and so he delayed his response by two days to consult with his corps commanders. This pause gave Rommel another opportunity on which to capitalize. He wedged open a bigger corridor through the Gazala Line and personally led supply columns back through to replenish the 15th Panzer Division.

British losses again mounted: 3,000 troops captured and 100 more tanks destroyed.

Before continuing farther north, Rommel considered the option of turning his tanks around to finish off Bir Hacheim. Rommel asked Bayerlein his opinion about taking Bir Hacheim. As Bayerlein described in *Rommel, the Desert Fox*: "I never liked this plan (of skirting the Gazala position around Bir Hacheim, then striking north) and, as Chief of Staff of the Afrika Korps, I told Rommel so continually. It seemed to me altogether too risky to go on without first knocking out Bir Hacheim. Six weeks before he asked me 'What would you do with your armor if you were General Ritchie?' I told him that I would keep it well away to the eastward, somewhere about El Adem (near Bir Hacheim), refuse battle at first and then strike at our flank when we were inside the Gazala position. 'You're crazy,' he said, 'they'll never do that!' though it was just what he would have done himself."

Bir Hacheim was staunchly defended by about 3,600 Free French troops, who fought valiantly to

A sentry stands watch beside a disabled truck. In the Cauldron, attacks could come from any direction at any time. When the British assaults commenced, Rommel noted that the guns of his tanks were firing *from three sides* toward the advancing British. *National Archives*

keep this southernmost, and probably most important box, from falling. After it succumbed to overwhelming Axis forces, Rommel wrote in his journal that it was one of the toughest battles he'd seen in Africa. A high compliment to the French soldiers who fought there.

Now he was free to wheel northward through the disintegrating Gazala Line, crushing successive boxes as he went. Masterful tactics evened the odds against the superior new Grant tanks. By mid-June, there was nothing left of the line except charred tank hulls, empty slit trenches and the ruins of each Allied stronghold.

Now, odds were even greater in his favor. He had twice the number of tanks the British had, probably the only time he had such an advantage. A considerable turnabout in odds from the first siege of Tobruk.

Finally, Tobruk Is Seized

The main defense of Tobruk—the Gazala Line—had fallen. Tobruk itself was not nearly such a strong, self-contained fortress as it had been in March 1941, when Rommel first attacked it.

Plus, overall British strength in the Middle East had dwindled, because of the drain on troops and equipment diverted eastward to meet the Japanese threat. Left in charge of Tobruk's garrison was South African Major General H. B. Klopper, a newcomer to North Africa.

A twin set of 105-millimeter light field howitzers (one in foreground, one in background) are pulled into position by Krauss-Maffei half-tracked prime movers before the capture of Tobruk. Devastating artillery and Luftwaffe bombardment, which began at 5:20 A.M. on June 20, 1942, are credited with setting off a chain reaction of minefield explosions that opened wide Tobruk's defenses for the infantry and tanks to storm the old fortress. *National Archives*

On May 30, 1942, British prisoners are evacuated on trucks inland to Acroma. *National Archives*

British Commonwealth prisoners of the South African Division are marched to containment on June 16, 1942. The division was encircled at Gazala. *National Archives*

Klopper's 35,000 troops were well aware of Rommel's approach, as box after box fell on the path that led inevitably to Tobruk. As if an African elephant were stomping toward them, they worked feverishly to bolster their defenses. They laid mines and extended their patrols outward from Tobruk about 30 miles.

The advancing tanks quickly ravaged the outlying defenses and Ritchie allowed the troops there to retreat toward the Egyptian frontier. Then, the last extended line of defense for Tobruk fell.

By June 18, 1942, Rommel moved in to take his prize. Italo-German forces massed outside the perimeter and surrounded the city. On June 20, the Luftwaffe pounded it mercilessly in 580 sorties, then the Afrika Korps and XX Italian Corps attacked with a mind-numbing barrage of artillery.

In his firsthand account of *Panzer Battles*, von Mellenthin stated: "The combined weight of the artillery and bombing was terrific." In the final assault, Rommel's infantry charged with fixed bayonets following the shelling in the World War I fashion described in *Infanterie Greift an*.

With the outcome certain, Klopper gave the order to destroy thousands of tons of precious stores that had been stockpiled to feed Ritchie's own offensive. But the supplies were so vast that Klopper's troops couldn't blow it up fast enough.

When Tobruk surrendered at 9:40 A.M. on June 21, great quantities of materiel remained. Not only did Rommel win the vital port and silence the guns that had regularly harassed his advance into Egypt, he won 30 tanks and more than 2,000 other vehicles, along with artillery guns, shells, and precious gasoline.

The reward for this victory was an immediate promotion to field marshal. In reaction, Rommel confided to his wife: "I would much rather he had given me one more division."

With Tobruk secured, Rommel set up defensive positions along the coast. *National Archives*

Chapter Six

DESERT ARMAGEDDON

Rommel's army had surged 600 miles east, in two equal lunges of approximately 300 miles each. Now, he was a mere 60 miles short of Alexandria.

As he loomed over the fortress of El Alamein, pandemonium ensued in Alexandria and Cairo. It looked as if, this time, Rommel might reach the lofty objective of capturing the two largest Egyptian cities. Anticipating the invasion, citizens in both cities fled in droves by any transportation available in any direction that would avoid the path of the Axis advance.

Auchinleck left Cairo, too. But instead he flew into harm's way, and without any thought of retreat. He stopped first at Mersa Matruh, on June 25. There he dismissed Ritchie from his command of the Eighth Army. Rommel had humbled yet another enemy commander. How many faced him in North Africa and were consequently relieved or captured? Six in all:

> *"A few more divisions for my Army, with supplies for them guaranteed, would have sufficed to bring about the complete defeat of the entire British forces in the Near East. But it was not to be. With only three German divisions, whose fighting strength was often ludicrously small, we kept the British army busy in Africa for 18 long months and gave them many a trouncing, until our strength finally ran out at Alamein."*
>
> —Erwin Rommel

Wavell, Neame, O'Connor, Cunningham, Ritchie, and (unaware at this time) Auchinleck himself.

Stalemate at El Alamein

Auchinleck assumed personal command of the British forces. He then consolidated his forces in the western-most pockets, moving them from Mersa Matruh east to El Alamein.

El Alamein was already well fortified in anticipation of this British consolidation. It was the place best suited to make a stand. The natural terrain made it defensible. To the north was the Mediterranean Sea and to the south was the Qattara Depression, which was an almost impassable area of salt marshes and quicksand.

Throughout July and half of August, Auchinleck lived like Rommel—in the midst of his troops, eating the same monotonous, meager food they ate, sleeping under open sky as they slept. In this way Auchinleck hoped to boost the morale of the Eighth Army, while

General Sir Harold Alexander is chosen by Churchill as the next Middle East commander in chief, replacing Auchinleck. Churchill knew Britain needed a victory soon and his conclusion was that Auchinleck could not deliver it. Alexander's appointment resulted partly because Auchinleck's cable to London in July 1942 insisted upon a great infusion of equipment before another offensive—a whopping 50-percent increase of tanks for *reserve*. It evoked a famous Churchill quip: "This was an almost prohibitive condition. Generals only enjoy such comforts in Heaven. And those who demand them do not always get there!" (Churchill: Vol. III) *National Archives*

benefiting from firsthand observation of his army's strengths and weaknesses, and orchestrating changes to improve them.

At the same time, Rommel pounded away at El Alamein with as much ferocity as his gasoline and ammunition stores allowed. But Auchinleck's equally fierce determination and talent for tactics thwarted Rommel repeatedly. The German offensive had reached a standstill.

English war correspondent Alaric Jacob was there in July 1942. In Harold Elk Straubing's *A Taste of War,* Jacob described the battle of El Alamein as "... raging with unabated fury, but so far without a decision. The tired Axis troops were being pounded all the time from the air and blasted incessantly by our guns. Directly before me the flashes of our guns were like so many matches being struck in quick succession on the sandy plateau . . . the sharper, more staccato crack of antitank guns rose now and then above the general rumble of the battle."

Another Change in British Command

A stalemate at El Alamein wasn't good enough for Churchill. As the Eighth Army's morale had sagged through the defeats of early summer, so did British public opinion as a whole. Churchill was very sensitive to the mood of the public. He realized during the summer of 1942 that there weren't many heroes to cheer about on the British homefront. The army's masterstroke over the Italian desert forces the year before was all but forgotten.

To fill the void, an odd thing happened among the British people. Lacking a hero of their own, the British developed a begrudging and odd hero worship of their archenemy's champion, Erwin Rommel. There was a hint of reverence and awe in British newspapers. Even the parlance among British desert troops included a laudatory "You did a Rommel!" if someone did something well.

Churchill decided there was only one solution. He erased the chalkboard of leadership in his desert army

The man who would lead the overwhelming charge against Rommel: General, and later Field Marshal, Bernard Law Montgomery. Much like Rommel in certain ways, far different in other ways, Montgomery also saw combat in World War I. He distinguished himself when, as a young lieutenant, he was struck by sniper fire after taking the French village of Meteren. He lay in the street in a pool of blood the rest of the day with another sniper victim sprawled dead on top of him. Pinned down by fire, his own troops were unable to come to his aid until nightfall. After he was carried to the rear, "... the doctors reckoned I could not live and, as the [Advanced Dressing Station] was shortly to move, a grave was dug for me," Montgomery wrote in his memoirs. But a surprised doctor detected a faint heartbeat as the station was closing down and the grave went unfilled. When Montgomery awoke in England, he found he'd been promoted to captain and awarded the DSO. *Dwight D. Eisenhower Library*

COMMANDER-IN-CHIEF IN THE MIDDLE EAST

1.   Your prime and main duty will be to take or destroy at the earliest opportunity the German-Italian Army commanded by Field-Marshal Rommel, together with all its supplies and establishments in Egypt and Libya.

2.   You will discharge or cause to be discharged such other duties as pertain to your Command without prejudice to the task described in paragraph 1, which must be considered paramount in His Majesty's interests.

Churchill's directive

to Alexander is to vanquish, once and for all, Rommel's forces. The fact that Rommel is identified by name illustrates the very personal nature of the desert war for Churchill. (The document was preserved for use in the movie "Desert Victory," released through 20th *Century Fox.)*

and started over. Then he wrote in two new names: General Sir Harold Alexander, who replaced Auchinleck as commander-in-chief of the Middle East, and Lieutenant General Bernard Law Montgomery, who assumed command of the Eighth Army.

Montgomery was to become the hero who was so badly needed by British citizens and their demoralized troops. Rommel could not know what this change of British leadership would mean for him. Montgomery was an unknown to him and the German High Command.

Rommel still had the utmost faith in his troops, his own abilities, and his own destiny. Another change of command by the enemy did not change that. His writing during the time didn't dwell on Montgomery, but it did dwell on the entry of the United States into the war. "By declaring war on America," Rommel wrote, "We had brought the entire American industrial potential into the service of the Allied war production. We in Africa knew all about the quality of its achievements. I obtained for myself some figures on American productive capacity. It was many times greater than ours."

The United States was in the midst of full mobilization—turning all of its considerable resources toward the war effort. He fully understood that the products of American industrial might would now be aimed squarely at Germany. That summer, he began to see examples firsthand in the desert: The Grant and Sherman tanks; the Priest self-propelled gun; a profusion of Willys and Ford jeeps. And next would come American troops to join with the men of the British Commonwealth in overwhelming numbers. While the Allied forces grew greater and stronger in every way, the finite resources of Rommel's own forces became more and more apparent.

Rommel vs. Montgomery

There are striking differences and similarities between Rommel and Montgomery. Both were infantry veterans of World War I, but they had seen different types of fighting. Unlike Rommel, who had spent most of his time on the Italian front, Montgomery had experienced the mass butchery of meat-grinder assaults in France. The waste of those fruitless assaults made him want to avoid the static actions that characterized the first Great War. A heavy artillery barrage, followed by an infantry assault spread across a wide front meant guaranteed death for tens of thousands of soldiers.

On the battlefield, Montgomery was cautious and calculating, whereas Rommel regularly took tremendous risks. Montgomery won battles by overwhelming his enemy with massed attacks at precise points. Rommel used agile movement, deception, and surprise. Montgomery spent great amounts of time in meticulous planning loaded with detail to prepare for any contingency, and then he carried out the plan without deviation. Rommel created a broad-brush plan, but then relied on acrobatic maneuver and improvisation to guide his movements as the battle ebbed and flowed. Because Rommel almost always commanded forces that were outnumbered, his methods worked well. And because Montgomery commanded larger, well-supplied forces, his style was effective for his army.

Rommel was four years younger than Montgomery, who was born in 1887. Neither came from families with money or social status. Neither family had a military tradition. So, like Rommel, Montgomery moved up through the class-conscious officer ranks by sheer skill, discipline, and ambition. In the years between the world wars, both remained line officers and concentrated on developing their leadership abilities and battle tactics. Both were extraordinarily competitive, even aggressive toward their colleagues. Montgomery once admitted, "One had to be a bit of a cad to succeed in the army. I am a bit of a cad." Neither had much interest in anything outside the realm of the military.

A machine gunner atop an armored car fires into the skies over Cyrenaica. Increasingly, British fighters swarmed over German positions, as RAF squadrons were reconstituted in exclusive support of the Eighth Army. On August 30, 1942, *500* RAF sorties were flown. *National Archives*

A lethal 88 trained on vast sands before it. Its crew stands at leisure awaiting targets on the eastern horizon. *National Archives*

Both were completely devoted to their wives. When Montgomery's wife died before the war, it was a grevious loss that caused him to vow never to marry again. Rommel, of course, maintained almost daily correspondence with his wife and visited as frequently as possible.

Montgomery's personality was not a pleasant one. Arrogant and ruthless, he commanded with cold competence. He did not possess the charismatic appeal of Rommel.

Both struggled with their superiors. But both were professionals, highly skilled and completely committed to their mission.

And so it was that the image of Montgomery with his trademark beret embellished with its two armored brigade badges, and that of Rommel with his goggles and binoculars, would become famous the world over.

On August 13, 1942 (the anniversary of the great victory at Blenheim, as Churchill pointed out), Montgomery took over Ritchie's post in command of the Eighth Army. As Montgomery recalled in his memoirs, " . . . orders from Alexander were quite simple; they were to destroy Rommel and his army."

Rommel's Setback at Alam el Halfa

As night fell on August 30, Rommel considered making a go-for-broke last attempt to bulldoze through British positions and charge into the heart of Egypt.

It amounted to a lopsided contest between Montgomery's superior manpower, equipment, air power and fortified positions, and Rommel's iron will to break through.

Montgomery was well supported by the RAF, which committed 525 planes to support him. On the ground he had, among an armada of vehicles, 84 new six-pound antitank guns, which was comparable to the deadly German 88s. Overall, Montgomery held an almost two-to-one superiority in antitank weaponry and artillery. Montgomery had a total of 1,029 tanks (210

During a lull, a German driver has opened the hood of his vehicle to let heat escape. In the background is an 88-millimeter gun and its crew. *National Archives*

Instead of its innovative role in the desert as an antitank gun, this German 88-millimeter is turned skyward for its original use as an antiaircraft gun. Both U.S. Army Air Forces and Royal Air Force owned the sky in the last stages of the desert war. *National Archives*

The crew commander and observer watch *as 88-millimeter shells shriek downrange on the battlefield with pinpoint accuracy. The observer gauged effect and the commander shouted adjustments of aim to the crew. With the onslaught of Allied forces, they grew fewer and fewer and, by November 2, 1942, only one-third of the German guns (including the precious 88s) remained, and those continued their deadly duties to the end.* National Archives

A British Matilda smolders after an 88 scored a direct hit. *Rommelarchiv*

of which were the new Grant tanks built in America) to Rommel's 500 (327 of those were inferior Italian tanks). Montgomery's troop strength was 195,000 compared to Rommel's 104,000.

Not only were Rommel's forces feeble in comparison to Montgomery's, but Rommel himself was in poor health—exhausted and sick with jaundice and intestinal disorders. He had become so weak he could hardly climb in and out of his *Mammut*. He did his best to hide this weakness from his troops and continued to push himself mercilessly.

War correspondent Alaric Jacob commented in *A Taste of War*: "I thought of the prediction an important German prisoner had made the day before: 'Rommel has wonderful energy himself but he drives us too hard

and some of us can't take much more of this. Rest we must have soon.'" This statement is a glimpse at how hard Rommel was pushing himself and his troops, as well as the image he projected to the front-line soldier—inexhaustible energy, incapable of fatigue, impervious. However, this image was a false one.

Compounding the weakness of his smaller forces was a lack of supplies. Ammunition, gasoline and other materiel were trickling in to Axis-held ports now that the British had seized back control of the Mediterranean.

Rommel was, in part, to blame for the precarious supply situation. His own personal influence had caused Hitler to delay Operation Hercules, the assault on Malta. That delay had allowed British forces to reinforce the strategic island stronghold and beat back

As the United States moved toward full mobilization of industry, a profusion of American vehicles and weapons of all types filled out the ranks in the British Eighth Army. "From the moment that the overwhelming industrial capacity of the United States could make itself felt in any theater of war," Rommel wrote, "there was no longer any chance of ultimate victory in that theater." Here, a Sherman medium tank lurches over the dunes in the vicinity of El Alamein. The Sherman had a cast hull (versus a welded hull like most others) and a 75-millimeter gun. *National Archives*

The aftermath of battle: Sand littered with guns, ration boxes, spent shells. *Rommelarchiv*

More and more devastating news reaches Rommel as the retreat west continues. In the early afternoon of November 3, Rommel received the stunning message from *Der Fuhrer* that began, "In the situation in which you find yourself, there can be no other thought but to stand fast. . . ." By November 4, a total troop strength of 22,000 remained. *National Archives*

Axis forces in the Mediterranean. That Allied resurgence contributed to his supply problems now.

If supplies did make it through the perilous sea journey, then they still had to be transported great distances from the ports to his fighting troops. He was now 300 miles from Tobruk, 600 miles from Benghazi and 1,200 miles from Tripoli. The bottom line was that Rommel had not even a third of the supplies needed to wage the attack he had planned.

Based on excellent intelligence, Montgomery knew all of this. British intelligence estimates of Axis troop and tank strength were very accurate. Rommel's poor health condition was even known, as were his struggles with Berlin and Rome. The British had done their homework.

Like the master of a deadly chess game, Montgomery had carefully studied all the options open to Rommel and to himself. No matter which way Rommel moved, Montgomery had prepared a response.

Rommel basically had two options for his attack, neither of which looked promising. One possibility was to fight through the heavily mined sector north of Ruweisat Ridge. The other, equally unsavory option was an end-run around the southern end of the El Alamein Line. There were mines there too, but at least the end-run was a proven maneuver that had served Rommel well previously in the desert war, like the sweep around the south of Bir Hacheim in May 1942. Even though the odds were against him, that maneuver might afford him a small advantage of tactical experience. It had worked before when the odds seemed stacked against him.

His plan became a hybrid between the two options: He would make a feint at Ruweisat Ridge, then veer off to sweep south of the El Alamein Line.

With his usual confidence, Rommel ordered his clanking behemoth of four armored divisions to begin rolling toward the center of Ruweisat Ridge on August 30, 1942, at 10 P.M. The massed approach toward the center was a thinly veiled diversion. As they neared the ridge, his leading tanks veered south to begin their sweep around. The 15th and 21st Panzer Divisions of the Afrika Korps were to chisel away at defenses in the south and, once past the British minefields, they were to turn left, pause, and make a great arc that would skirt the southern end of the El Alamein Line and encircle the enemy. Rommel chose his point of entry and route based on the fairly reliable aerial intelligence provided by the Luftwaffe.

Once an avenue was opened, he could use the Qattara Depression to his advantage. In the impassable void of the depression, there would be no massed enemy assaults to threaten his right flank.

But Rommel expected too much of his outnumbered forces and too little from the well-entrenched enemy and its cerebral leader. Trouble began immediately with delays in clearing the minefields before the morning light. The minefield was larger than expected. Plus, the deep, soft sand of the region slowed the progress of his panzer regiments. Dust storms began and blew with such fury that direction became confused and some elements became separated.

Eventually, after surmounting the obstacles of the minefields and the wind and the darkness, Rommel broke through. But in typical fashion, he improvised. Based on what he sensed was happening as his troops moved forward, Rommel reevaluated his plan and turned his forces on a northward course earlier than expected. Now, directly ahead of his panzers was yet another ridge—Alam el Halfa Ridge where, again, the enemy was well prepared.

Alam el Halfa Ridge, 25 miles northeast of the Qattara Depression, was where the Eighth Army and its new commander would clash head on with the Germans.

In his memoirs, Montgomery recounts, "I decided to hold the Alam Halfa Ridge strongly with the 44th Division and to locate my tanks just south of its western end. The strictest orders were issued that the armor was not to be loosed against Rommel's forces; it was not to move; the enemy was to be allowed to beat up against it and to suffer heavy casualties. It was obvious to me that Rommel could not just by-pass my forces and go off eastward to Cairo; if he did, I could have descended on his rear with 400 tanks and that would have been the end of his army."

Montgomery planned for this possible shift. In fact, he hoped for it: His American-made Grant tanks lay in wait. Hell's fury opened up on the approaching German columns. A barrage rained down from hidden British artillery, the Grant tanks began firing and, most of all, the RAF swarmed overhead. RAF fighter-bombers flew 500 sorties that day, with American squadrons in support. The Allies owned the skies and the Axis forces could not even get through to deliver badly needed fuel for the tanks.

Rommel's regiments were fragmented, and communication between units broke down. German and Italian tanks were being picked off by aircraft and unseen artillery on the ridge.

Rommel and his men fought back with the ferocity of a cornered animal, and with some success. But before it was over, he had lost 49 irreplaceable tanks.

Beginning on September 2, Rommel decided to cut his losses, regroup and pull back. By September 6, the Axis survivors had returned to the refuge of their own lines.

The mauling of Axis forces that occurred on the sandy undulations between Himeimat and Alam el Halfa was a great psychological boost for the British. True, they had not crushed the Panzerarmee completely. And, in terms of sheer numbers, the British lost approximately equal numbers of men and tanks as the Germans (proportionately, with the British enjoying a nearly 2-to-1 advantage, losses were far greater for Rommel). But all elements of the British forces—artillery and infantry troops, pilots and tank crews—worked together like a well-oiled, synchronized fighting machine. The troops were quick to recognize that

The sun sets on the Axis in North Africa. Rommel withdrew to Tunisia, where another onslaught awaited him: The Anglo-American forces that had landed on November 8, 1942, in northwest Africa. Twilight had come. *National Archives*

Montgomery's planning and insistence on training and discipline had paid off.

It was a psychological victory for British troops in the field and the public on the homefront, because now they clearly had a military leader who was a match for the Desert Fox. For the Axis, it was decidedly a grievous blow. It became unmistakably clear that the Allies would only grow stronger and stronger, because they had superior equipment in the form of American-made tanks, trucks and aircraft, coming into North Africa in great numbers.

The Great Deceiver Is Deceived

Montgomery did not pursue the retreating Panzerarmee. This left Rommel perplexed but relieved. Instead, Montgomery held back, intent on preparing for the Armageddon that he hoped would crush Rommel once and for all.

Finally safe behind the lines on September 4, an exhausted Rommel collapsed into bed after a week on the run. He was long past the point of needing simple medical treatment and required nothing less than hospitalization. He suffered from nasal diphtheria, a chronic stomach condition, and poor circulation. But he stubbornly refused to leave his troops in the desert.

Equally stubborn in his own way, Montgomery insisted on taking his time and refused to continue the offensive before October. It didn't matter whether Churchill himself demanded a September offensive. Montgomery said, "If a September attack was ordered . . . they would have to get someone else to do it."

For the British, the commander had proven himself to his troops. But the victory at Alam el Halfa Ridge was not enough to prove the battle readiness of the troops to their commander. Montgomery resolved to craft his Eighth Army into an unbeatable legion. He started with the basics and went about the task with the same methodical skill exhibited in his battle plan for Alam el Halfa Ridge.

Simultaneous with this stepped up training, he went to work on constructing a large-scale deception to fool Rommel. Under the direct leadership of Lieutenant Colonel Charles Richardson, plans were drawn up to dupe the Germans into believing that the British would launch an offensive at the southern part of the El Alamein line. In reality, Montgomery's plan was to attack in the north, where Rommel's strongest positions were.

Knowing that the watchful eyes of the Luftwaffe and Italian air reconnaissance would be on them, the British constructed several fake heavy artillery regiments. From the air, wood poles and canvas appeared as armor and cannon barrels. The focal point of the deception was

a dummy water pipeline, constructed of empty petrol cans, that extended for 20 miles southward. Phantom supply dumps were set up along the pipeline route, all with the pretense that a vast army would be moving in this direction to wage a major battle.

The pace of the construction was all part of Richardson's magnificent and complex ruse to make Axis observers believe that the offensive would not begin until mid-November, after the pipeline had reached its southernmost point.

At the same time, Montgomery stashed days worth of food, gasoline, and ammunition in desert cisterns. Supplies were secretly transported and concealed in the north. Food supplies and ammunition were trucked in at night and set under camouflaged nets. 2,000 tons of gasoline came in on the coastal railroad. Tanks, disguised with canvas to look like empty trucks heading back for supplies, rolled to assembly areas in the north.

Sickness, Fatigue, Impaired Judgment

Rommel's medical advisor, Dr. Forster, and his chief of staff, General Gauss, communicated to the German High Command that, because of Rommel's worsening health, he was unfit for command.

Rommel wanted General Heinz Guderian, an early proponent of armored operations and leader of the 1939 Polish invasion, as his temporary replacement. But Berlin would not agree to this and Rommel remained in the desert until another suitable commander could be found. General Georg Stumme, a veteran of the Russian front, eventually arrived to assume command. Although Rommel was less than thrilled with Stumme, who had no experience in desert warfare, he finally flew back to Germany on September 23 for hospitalization.

At the same time, most of the Afrika Korps veteran officers were also ailing and being replaced. A letter to Frau Rommel dated September 9, 1942, notes that: "Now Gauss is unfit for tropical service and has to go away for six months. Things are not looking too good with Westphal, he's got liver trouble [jaundice]. Lieutenant Colonel von Mellenthin is leaving today with amebic dysentery, so that every divisional commander and the corps commander have changed inside 10 days."

Rommel's hospitalization came at a critical time and he knew it. It meant he was out of action in the face of an imminent enemy offensive.

Climactic Showdown at El Alamein

Montgomery chose the night of October 23 to launch the offensive. Even as British armor was moving toward the northern lines en masse and the RAF was winging its way from airfields in the east, Stumme was

Before the Anglo-American landings in North Africa, General Dwight D. Eisenhower arrives in England. He set as the objective forming "the best army that the United States has ever put in the field." *Dwight D. Eisenhower Library*

completely unaware. The Germans had been completely fooled by the British fakery, especially the false water pipeline, which begged for notice, pointing like a giant finger to an advance in the south. Plus, based on the progress of the pipeline, the Germans felt that surely there would be no offensive until November.

The British attack, called Operation Lightfoot, started with the distant drone of aircraft engines at 9:30 P.M., as RAF bombers approached their targets—northern strongholds on the El Alamein Line and Axis airfields to the rear. Simultaneously, Allied artillery opened fire with 900 guns blasting in unison.

Explosions, panic, and chaos were the result. Artillery shells and aerial bombs set off acres of mines in front of Axis positions, causing a deafening, mind-numbing crescendo of blasts unparalleled since World War I. The explosions completely severed

communications lines and German headquarters was instantly cut off from every front-line unit.

Stumme bolted for his staff car. He motioned for Colonel Buchting, one of his officers, to accompany him in the car and then barked an order for the driver to head for the front. Shells exploded all around them as they swerved to and fro across the desert sands. Amidst the flashes and roar of the explosions, Stumme's car suddenly was riddled by machine gun fire. The ambush came from an advancing unit of the Australian infantry. Buchting fell forward immediately, mortally wounded. Stumme began clutching his chest, although no wound was visible.

The driver had no time to worry about his passengers. He slammed the car in reverse to avoid the piercing hail of bullets. But Stumme, now in the throes of a massive heart attack, struggled from the car seat and

A U.S. half-track rumbles through Tunisia. After Eisenhower's successful landing in Operation Torch, Churchill wrote about North Africa: "Before Alamein we never had a victory. After Alamein we never had a defeat." (Churchill: Vol. IV) *National Archives*

gripped the door handle to get out of the vehicle, then he fell dead. The driver was captured and Stumme's fate would remain a mystery for days. While the British pressed their unexpected attack, the Panzerarmee was without a leader. German headquarters did not know what happened to Stumme, only that he had disappeared.

Word reached Hitler, who personally urged Rommel to return to command. Two days after the offensive was launched, Rommel flew back to Africa. As soon as he was on the ground, he met with General Wilhelm von Thoma, who had assumed command of the Panzerarmee in Stumme's absence. The news was grave: the Afrika Korps had only enough gasoline for three days of fighting.

To Rommel, this news was nearly as stunning as the concussion of a real shell. On a visit to Hitler's headquarters in East Prussia a few weeks before, *Der Fuhrer* had assured him of the "secret weapons" the Nazi regime had under development and the vast fleets of tanks he would send to Africa. Hitler rambled on about fictional shallow-depth ferries that would shuttle fuel across the Mediterranean Sea and 40 new Tiger tanks earmarked for Rommel's armies.

Rommel now stood hollow-eyed. Through the great ups and downs of the desert war, Rommel's faith in Hitler's word had remained intact. At that very moment, seeing the shambles his command had become, perhaps for the first time Rommel came to a realization that *Der Fuhrer* was not in touch with reality.

Perhaps too, Rommel fully accepted the futility of his army's situation. Two days after he returned to the African front, he wrote to Frau Rommel: "A very hard struggle. No one can conceive the burden that lies on me."

Hard-hit units like the 15th Panzer Division were at a quarter of their full strength. The 15th had been located along the supposedly safe northern part of the German lines, and had lost 88 of its 119 tanks. Rommel immediately went about shoring up the weakening defense. He even launched counterattacks, but to no avail.

Despite the devastation inflicted on the Axis, Montgomery was not satisfied with his army's progress. After several days of ferocious fighting, his units were not reaching objectives as quickly as he ordered his commanders to achieve them.

He was bent on annihilating the Panzerarmee. Remote and academic, he retired alone into his trailer and closed the door. Later, he emerged with Operation Supercharge, which was a plan for a new thrust. He would concentrate the Allied assault in the north, where Australian units had made excellent headway. He would push through at that point and take over the German-controlled part of the coastal road to completely sever

the vein of Rommel's barely pulsing supply line, leaving the Panzerarmee with none of its lifeblood—fuel.

Rommel was aware of the Australians' reputation as fierce fighters and he saw the success they were now having against his units. Where they had penetrated, he ordered the 90th Light Division forward from reserve. He also ordered the 21st Panzer Division, 30 miles to the south, to move into the northernmost position of the line. Even as he uttered the order, it must have caught in his throat, because he knew that it was a one-way journey. There was no chance of going back once the order was executed, because lack of fuel would not allow a retreat to the south or anywhere else. But in the dark moments of desperation, Rommel had no alternative but to halt the British assault in the north with every bit of his remaining resources.

In another chess-like move, Montgomery shifted his main assault south about 5 miles when he realized that Rommel was repositioning his forces. Montgomery left the Australians fighting in the north. But he aimed his new attack at a weak seam where the German and Italian forces joined on the line.

The new plan was to break through with New Zealand and British infantry all the way to an undeveloped road called the Rahman Track, where the Axis artillery was concentrated. Montgomery hoped this would be the final blow for Rommel's army.

The renewed offensive commenced at 1 A.M. on November 2, 1942. It started like the initial assault, with a devastating artillery barrage to soften defenses and eliminate Axis minefields. Thanks to accurate shelling, the British and New Zealand infantry advanced on its objective by early the next morning. And, as planned, their tanks bypassed them and continued toward the Rahman Track.

As the sun began to rise at their backs, the British tanks were silhouetted perfectly against the horizon. Rommel was in the process of quickly positioning anti-tank guns in their path. The German 88s and field artillery opened fire with a vengeance.

An hour later, 70 British tanks lay smoldering in the sand. Other armored brigades rolled forward to continue the push. Rommel ordered the 21st and 15th Panzer Divisions to blast at the advancing enemy from both sides. The bloody battle lasted until evening, when only 35 German tanks remained.

This left the remaining infantry helpless. As preserved in *The Foxes of the Desert*, Lieutenant Ralph Ringler of the 104th Panzer Grenadier Regiment wrote in his diary: "In Africa there was no such thing as close-in fighting with armor. We had no explosive charges or shrapnel. A Mark II made for my position. I crouched in terror in a corner. Would that squeaking noise of the tracks over my foxhole ever come to an end? When would the driver stop? As soon as he had passed I jumped to my feet. . . . The (British) C.O. was so sure of himself that he was looking out of the hatch. I pulled a hand grenade from my belt, drew the pin and threw it. It bounced against the turret and exploded with no effect. The tank commander grinned at me . . . Now he waved his arms as on firing practice: 'Near miss,' and drove on." Ringler went on to describe how the tank commander deliberately crushed other soldiers in their trenches.

Rommel witnessed the slaughter and issued orders for a disciplined retreat. Axis forces began the withdrawal that night, but the next morning Hitler's order arrived: "In the situation in which you find yourself, there can be no other thought but to stand fast, yield not a yard of room and throw every gun and man into battle. The utmost efforts are being made to help you. It would not be the first time in history that a strong will has triumphed over the bigger battalions. As to your troops, you can show them no other road than that to victory or death."

The order had been direct and left no room for interpretation, not even with the justification of a clearer picture from the firsthand vantage point. Rommel halted the retreat. But with losses numbering 32,000 troops and more than 450 tanks already, he fell into despair. Field Marshal Kesselring flew in that day and was witness to more bloodshed in what was clearly a futile effort.

With agreement from Kesselring, Rommel disobeyed *Der Fuhrer* and ordered a full retreat west. The next day, word came from Hitler authorizing the retreat.

No Safe Havens West

The withdrawal to Tunisia was the longest, most agonizing retreat of Rommel's life. His forces had been devastated as never before, with whole divisions reduced to as few as 10 tanks and *total* troop strength across all divisions at 7,500 men. As he fled Sollum and Halfaya on November 9, he was forced to leave behind a thousand vehicles bottlenecked in the passes, where the RAF had bombed the head of the column.

Despite the desperate circumstances, the retreat was highly disciplined and orderly. This tiny remaining group, outnumbered by at least 20 to 1, harassed the pursuing British at every step. The wary Montgomery overestimated the fighting strength of his enemy. Well aware of Rommel's unpredictability and success in counterattacks, Montgomery held back the leading edge of his forces when Rommel's men stopped to take up holding positions. The question at each stop became: Is he stopping to catch his breath—or is he setting up to launch a counteroffensive?

Always wanting overwhelming firepower, Montgomery would wait for trailing units to catch up to the front to give him a twofold, threefold, even tenfold superiority. But at each stop, before Montgomery could mass for an attack, Rommel would make another froglike jump to the west.

On top of this dismal situation for Rommel, he received confirmation of terrible news: on November 8, 1942, British and American forces had landed in northwest Africa. Operation Torch had begun.

Anglo-Americans En Masse: Operation Torch

The idea of Operation Torch was to catch the Axis forces in a squeeze play between the invasion forces coming from the west and the Eighth Army following closely at Rommel's heels from the east.

The immediate challenge for the invading Allies, led by Lieutenant General Eisenhower, had nothing to do with Rommel. The landings took place on the beaches of colonies held by the Vichy French. The three landing sites were at Algiers in western Algeria, and at Casablanca and Oran in Morocco. As a condition of France's defeat, the Vichy government was forced to pledge support of the Reich with its remaining armed forces. Eisenhower could not know whether the French forces in Africa would uphold this pledge, so he planned to the largest amphibious invasion to date. American and British vessels numbered 352 transports, with 171 warships in support.

There *was* heavy opposition to the landings on November 8, but the French finally surrendered on November 11. Once the Americans were on the African continent, they prepared for the push eastward.

One young American from Wisconsin, Otto Kasovic, was a mechanic in the 30th Signal Corps. His experience shows that the Americans, like the early arrivals of the Afrika Korps, weren't trained or prepared for North African conditions. He recalls, "They unloaded trucks off the ships by the hundreds. It became my job to take out the *heaters* on those trucks. And because of mechanical trouble they'd been having in the desert, they had me replace the light grease on the wheels with heavier."

Once ashore and organized for their desert journey, the Allies pressed on past Algeria to capture the Tunisian ports before Axis reinforcements arrived. But already on November 9, German troops, comprising a new panzer army under General von Arnim, were arriving from Sicily. The action that followed was a race to gain control of Tunisia.

The newly landed British First Army clawed eastward toward Tunis to prevent Axis consolidation

Victory is savored

as British and American troops link up after crushing the Desert Fox between them. The British Eighth Army and American First Army linked near Gafsa and Tunis, which closed the loop around the remaining Italo-German armies. National Archives

between the reinforcements arriving daily and Rommel's forces pushing west. The British reached Souk el Arba, 80 miles from Tunis, on November 16, but even with repeated offensives, they could go no further. Eventually Rommel was able to link up with von Arnim's forces.

In the meantime, Montgomery's Eighth Army continued pushing from the east. They eventually reached the Mareth Line, where Rommel's forces had set up a rear guard in defensible terrain. In *Many Kinds of Courage*, Gerard Hacquebard commented: "During Montgomery's visit he informed us that there was to be a 'sticky do' ahead. A 'sticky do' implies a coming ferocious battle. Our job was to break through the Mareth Line. It was held along a ridge of foothills about 300 feet high, and with a gradual slope. The approaches to the line had been seeded with what were estimated to be several hundred thousand mines. If you walk on one, off goes your leg. If a tank hits one, off go the tracks."

Kasserine Pass

While the Axis held Montgomery at bay on the Mareth Line, Rommel saw the opportunity for an offensive against the new arrivals in the west. In the Eastern Dorsal Mountains, where the Americans had taken up position, Rommel prepared for an assault. The 1st American Armored Division counterattacked and found themselves in a trap that cost them 46 tanks and more than 300 men. Reeling from its losses, the American unit retreated to Kasserine Pass.

The pass was a gateway to Tebessa and Thala, which Rommel set as crucial objectives because victory there might force the Allies back into Algeria. Rommel continued the assault, which caused heavy losses on the Americans in their first taste of combat against the Germans.

Famed war correspondent Ernie Pyle wrote about the U.S. troops in *Here Is Your War*, "Our army was a green army, and most of our Tunisian troops were in actual battle for the first time against seasoned troops and commanders. It would take us months of fighting to gain the experience our enemies started with."

The clash at the Kasserine Pass led to the loss of 3,000 Americans as prisoners of war. One of these men, Thearl Mesecher, a private in the 34th Division, wrote in his diary on February 17, 1943 (which was later preserved in *American Diaries of World War II*): " . . . an enemy tank appears at the head of the ravine with heavy guns pointing directly at us in our crouched position. We had a last-minute decision to make. We can surrender and be prisoners of war for the duration, or die a hero's death by firing on that tank. Had there

been a band, and had it struck up a patriotic military march, we probably would have fired. There was no band. We did not fire. It gives one a sickening feeling to hand over one's life, liberty, and pursuit of happiness to the enemy unconditionally."

The quick and surprising victories over the Americans renewed the old tactical genius within Rommel, and temporarily blotted out the dismal defeats of the past several months. In the heady air of triumph, he "felt like an old war horse that had heard music again." On the first night of battle, he ordered a bottle of champagne to celebrate. It would be a final, fleeting taste of victory for him.

He thrust forward again on February 19, 1943, but his personal struggles with rival German commanders crept back to haunt him. Von Arnim could have brought his newly arrived forces in to support Rommel's action, but he deliberately held back. Rommel turned to Rome for help, and von Arnim's forces were ordered into the battle. This allowed him to capture Kasserine Pass on February 20. But by February 22, the Allies sent reinforcements to block the rampaging panzers, and Rommel's short-lived advance was stopped.

In the *Eisenhower Diaries*, the entry for February 25, 1943, revealed that because the Allied commander had " . . . anticipation of a stalemate in that region . . . it became a definite possibility that some of Rommel's forces might try a quick combination with the enemy in Tunisia to deal us a damaging blow on the right flank."

But Rommel did not launch a flank attack on Eisenhower. Disappointed with the pace of the western battle, he broke off the engagement, which had reached a stalemate, and ordered his troops to turn and once again face the Eighth Army at the Mareth Line.

Soon after the victory at the Kasserine Pass, *Der Fuhrer* "offered" Rommel a position as supreme commander of Army Group Africa. This new command structure folded von Arnim's forces in with his. It would have been an arrangement beyond his wildest dreams at the outset of the desert war. But Rommel was fed up with the interference and lack of support Berlin had offered him, and he disgustedly turned down the position. He was formally appointed as Supreme Commander anyway.

With his increased forces, Rommel attacked on March 6, but Montgomery had been given the luxury of time to mass his forces and now he had four times the strength of the Axis. Rommel immediately realized his forces were hopelessly outnumbered and halted the offensive at the end of the first day.

He saw the hopelessness against such military might. He turned over command to von Arnim and flew directly to tell *Der Fuhrer* about the futile situation

German POWs *are herded by Americans guards. In Tunisia, more than 260,000 Axis troops were captured. Ernie Pyle noted in* Here Is Your War, *"I mingled with [German troops] all day and sensed no sadness among them. Theirs was not the delight of the Italians, but rather an acceptance of defeat in a war well fought . . ."*

in Africa. "He was unreceptive to my arguments and seemed to pass them all off with the idea that I had become a pessimist," Rommel recounted dismally.

Instead of listening to reason or listening to anything Rommel said, Hitler decorated him with the Iron Cross with oak leaves, swords and diamonds, then ordered him to remain in Germany, in secrecy. It was not common knowledge that Rommel had been relieved of command.

Inevitably, the German forces in Africa, numbering 200,000 men, reached a point where they could retreat no further. They found themselves completely surrounded by the middle of May 1943, and surrendered. The Axis threat in Africa finally was vanquished.

Ernie Pyle found himself among the hordes of German POWs in Tunisia. He wrote, "It made me a little light-headed to stand in the center of a crowd, the only American among scores of German soldiers, and not have to feel afraid of them. Their 88s stood abandoned. In the fields dead Germans still lay on the grass. By the roadside scores of tanks and trucks still burned."

In Germany, Rommel wrote, "Terrible as it was to know that . . . my men had found their way into Anglo-American prison camps, even more shattering was the realization that our star was in decline."

Had Rommel stayed in Africa, he would have been among the prisoners.

EPILOGUE

Rommel's ultimate fate—"forced suicide" on October 14, 1944—was rooted in the battle of El Alamein. According to Manfred Rommel, the general's only child (and a teenager during the war), his father's defiance of Hitler's order to halt the withdrawal from El Alamein to Tunis was the start of an irreparable conflict between the two men.

Manfred explained, "The Panzerarmee Afrika repeatedly received orders from Hitler to stop the retreat. Each time, my father paid no heed to these orders. In late November 1942, at the *Fuhrer's* headquarters, there was a clash between my father and Hitler, during which Hitler lost his composure and began to rave and rant. My father flew back to Libya and continued the retreat. . . . After the Italo-German troops were forced to surrender in Tunis (May 18, 1943), just as my father had predicted, Hitler summoned my father to *Der Fuhrer's* headquarters, to discuss the situation. My father stated to Hitler that he felt the war could not be won and recommended a change in the direction of war, to seek 'peace with conditions.' [Hitler] declared, according to my father, that he also knew that a German victory was no longer possible and added: 'Remember, nobody will make peace with me!'"

Manfred alone was privy to some of the actions and private thoughts of his father in the final weeks of his life. Father and son took long walks through the quaint hillside village of Herrlingen, where Rommel lived out the days before his death order was handed down from Hitler.

But Rommel had been given one last military assignment in the interlude after his return from Africa, but before his untimely end.

Defense of the Atlantic Wall

Despite the fact that Hitler never fully forgave the withdrawal from El Alamein, he attached Rommel to his staff in Berlin. It is clear that Hitler even considered appointing Rommel as commander of all Axis forces in the Italian Theater (this would have included Kesselring's forces). But on July 9, 1943, the Allies invaded Sicily. Mussolini was deposed later that month. The Allies brought the fight to the Italian peninsula on September 4, 1943, and Italy surrendered just four days later on September 8. It was decided not to send Rommel into another demanding battle.

Rommel continued suffering from a variety of physical ailments, some of them carryovers from the desert war, including terrible headaches, high blood

Rommel meets with Field Marshal Gerd von Rundstedt in March 1944. While the two field marshals disagreed on a strategy to meet the inevitable Allied invasion, both agreed that the Atlantic defenses were hopelessly inadequate. *Bundesarchiv*

pressure, insomnia, and rheumatism. Plus, he needed surgery for a ruptured appendix. When he recovered from that surgery in October 1943, General Alfred Jodl, now chief of operations at the German High Command, advised Hitler that Rommel was needed as tactical commander of the Atlantic Wall defenses, under the overall command of Field Marshal Gerd von Rundstedt.

By this time, it was certain that the Allies were planning an invasion across the English Channel into northwestern Europe. It was just a question of when and where. The vulnerable coastline extended 3,700 miles from Holland to the southern end of the Bay of Biscay.

Hitler did not agree to Rommel's appointment as tactical commander, but instead assigned him to the role of inspector general, with responsibility for inspecting the coastal defenses and reporting back directly about their readiness.

This role, which lasted two months, was uncomfortable at best. Rommel had responsibility, but no real authority to do much about the great inadequacies he found. Rommel saw the Atlantic defenses for the farce they were. He felt that the effort to arm the entire coastline was "a figment of Hitler's *wokenkuckucksheim* (cloud cuckoo land)." He told his son it was a bluff, "more for the German people than for the enemy."

Von Rundstedt was Germany's most senior field marshal and, at age 69, lacked the strength of will and body required to command an army. The old field marshal agreed with Rommel's deft assessment about the inadequacy of the defenses and actually welcomed Rommel's tactical expertise. On New Year's Eve 1943, Hitler finally accepted the recommendation to put Rommel in command of Army Group B, western Europe's most powerful forces, comprised of the 15th and 7th Armies, while von Rundstedt remained commander-in-chief. The two armies' defensive lines extended from Holland to the Loire River in southern France.

Defense of the coast was, at the very least, daunting, with challenges equal to those of the desert war, where the enemy consistently outnumbered him.

Rommel back in Germany. When Hitler summoned him to his headquarters soon after the Axis surrender in Tunis in May 1943, Rommel attempted to convince him that the only recourse was to seek "peace with conditions." Hitler disregarded the voice of reason and declared, "Remember, nobody will make peace with me!" *National Archives*

Disappointed, disillusioned, defeated, Rommel is left with the memory of North Africa. He knows now the bitterness of the vanquished, which he himself had inflicted on so many adversaries. *National Archives*

The expectation was for Rommel to construct an impregnable Atlantic wall. As he learned through his experiences as inspector general, no adequate defenses existed except at Calais, which was the narrowest point on the Channel coast and presumably the most likely place for an invasion. "Impregnable," by most definitions (including Rommel's) meant a death zone 6 miles deep that would prevent the establishment of any beachhead by the enemy.

Even though many in Germany viewed the war as a lost cause by the end of 1943, Rommel gave himself over completely to the new task. He took to the assignment with amazing enthusiasm, telling Frau Rommel that he would give it all he had. At that point, he must have had to reach deep within himself to find that drive, knowing firsthand the awesome strength possessed by the Allied forces.

His work on the Atlantic Wall was made harder by the fact that, as in Africa, the command structure was not clear. Rommel commanded Army Group B West, and only that. This did not include air units or any of the coastal defense forces of the German Navy. Nor did it include antiaircraft batteries or paratroops, which were part of the Luftwaffe.

Even command of the battle, once under way, was not decided. Hitler reserved control of the panzer

Rommel's villa, *as it appears today, on a winding hillside road renamed in the postwar years as "Erwin Rommel Street," in Herrlingen Germany.*

Author's collection

A bronze plaque at the front gate of the villa lists the occupants from 1906 through the present. Mingled subtly among the names is "Generalfeldmarschall Erwin Rommel." *Author's collection*

divisions for himself alone, despite the fact that Rommel was relying on them for the critical counterattack he knew would be needed on the first day after an invasion. And it was unclear which of the two Atlantic Wall commanders, von Rundstedt or Rommel, would actually control the battle.

D-Day

Lucie Rommel's birthday was June 6—a fateful coincidence. For months her husband had been anxious to spend a few days with her in Germany. Three days before her birthday, Rommel met with von Rundstedt in Paris, where both commanders agreed that conditions in the Channel and the weather (high winds, rain and unfavorable tides) made invasion unlikely. Plus, the Channel invasion was expected to coincide with the Red Army's summer offensive, which could not begin until after the late thaw in Poland. Rommel traveled from Paris (with a birthday present of handmade, gray suede shoes purchased there) to Herrlingen, where he would celebrate his wife's birthday.

The D-Day invasion came on June 6, 1944, with all the fury that the Allies could muster. In his absence,

Rommel's plan for counterattack never happened. Alone in command, von Rundstedt made the right decision to move two panzer divisions to the Normandy coast. But the panzers would not act on his words. Hitler had given them exclusive orders not to move except by his direct command. When von Rundstedt made a desperate call to Berlin to ask for this command, Jodl informed him that *Der Fuhrer* was still sleeping and could not be disturbed. Hitler was in bed until noon and the order finally came to move at 4 P.M. on June 6. It was already too late.

In the meantime, Rommel was speeding back to the Atlantic coast from Germany. Allied supremacy of the air made it impossible for him to fly. In the hours and days that followed, Eisenhower's forces established several beachheads and forged inland. The Allies breached the Atlantic Wall on the first day of the invasion.

The Purge

Rommel continued in command of Army Group B. But with the Allies entrenched on the continent, and their troops and supplies increasing exponentially every day, Germany was long past hope of victory and could only delay the inevitable.

Hitler tours field defenses with Rommel. The grand, impregnable defenses of the Atlantic wall existed only in Hitler's mind. Nothing Rommel (or anyone else) said convinced Hitler of the hopelessness against the impending Allied invasion. *National Archives*

Rommel's funeral procession through the streets of Ulm. It was a state funeral worthy of a hero, as Hitler promised; Hitler also followed through on his promise that Frau Rommel and son Manfred would not be harmed. *The Times* in London on October 16 ran an obituary of more than a thousand words, much of it inaccurate (e.g., propaganda hype like "Nazi party member from its beginning"). The circumstances of his death remained secret until after the war. *Bundesarchiv*

Germany's luck had run out and so had Rommel's. On July 16, 1944, while he was traveling between units in the countryside of Normandy, a British fighter (probably a Spitfire from a forward-based RAF squadron) swooped low and opened fire on his car. During two years on the front line of the desert war—through bullets, bombing, shelling, and exploding mines—Rommel had many close calls, but was never seriously wounded. Now in the back seat of his open staff car, he heard the whine of the diving aircraft as it aligned with the road for a strafing run. As the British pilot poured out a well-placed stream of lead, the stricken vehicle sped out of control and crashed. Among many other wounds, Rommel's skull was fractured in three places, including a crushed cheekbone that impaired his vision in the left eye. Even his greatest honor, the *Pour le Mérité* worn closely around his neck, was damaged. He wrote to Frau Rommel,

Tributes to Rommel continue to be left by his grave. This etched plaque has been left by an "American tanker" more than a half-century after American forces under Eisenhower engaged Rommel in Tunisia. *Author's collection*

Rommel's grave as it looks today in St. Andreas' churchyard. It is situated in the cool shadows of tall trees on the churchyard's terraces. The lush vegetation surrounding it includes heather, which blooms year-round (this photo was taken in February 1998). In the lower right corner is the grave of his wife, Frau Lucie Rommel. *Author's collection*

149

The steeple of St. Andreas Church in Herrlingen today. Rommel was laid to rest in the churchyard on October 19, 1944. *Author's collection*

"My left eye is still closed and swollen, but the doctors say it will get better. My head is still giving me a lot of trouble at night, though I feel very much better in the daytime."

While Rommel lay in a hospital recovering, the wheels had already been set in motion for a cataclysmic plan. Germans were plotting to assassinate Hitler and avert the total destruction of their nation.

The plan was simple. On July 20, 1944, the plot's leader, Colonel Klaus von Stauffenberg was to plant a time bomb in a briefcase at Hitler's headquarters in East Prussia. He successfully planted the bomb in a conference room and left under the pretense of making a phone call, but the plan went awry. The bomb exploded, killing and maiming many in the room, but a heavy oak table largely shielded Hitler from the blast.

Hitler's retaliation was beyond brutal, even by the standards of justice in the Third Reich. Hitler's Gestapo tracked down every lead to find anyone even remotely connected with the plotters. The plan had originated with a small group of prominent German politicians and high-ranking military officers. However, nearly 7,000 people were arrested and some 5,000 were killed—the vast majority of whom had no active part, nor even knowledge, of the plan.

Rommel played no role in planning the assassination, but he did have knowledge. He did not know the particulars, like when, where, and how, but he did know that a plot was afoot. He also did not know how large a role the plotters had planned for *him* if the plot succeeded. Under torture, some conspirators revealed that they had hopes of Rommel assuming leadership of Germany once Hitler was dead.

Hitler appointed von Rundstedt as president of the Court of Honor that would hand down judgment on those suspected. He was very severe, and his actions drew criticism (privately) from his peers in the officer corps. "If I had not (been harsh)," von Rundstedt explained later, "I too might have been considered a traitor." The judgment handed down for Rommel came directly from Hitler.

On October 14, 1944, two generals from the Army Personnel Branch, Wilhelm Burgdorf and Ernst Maisel, came to the doorstep of Rommel's home in

Today, many Rommel artifacts are displayed in the Rommelarchiv, housed on the first floor of Herrlingen's civic building. *Author's collection*

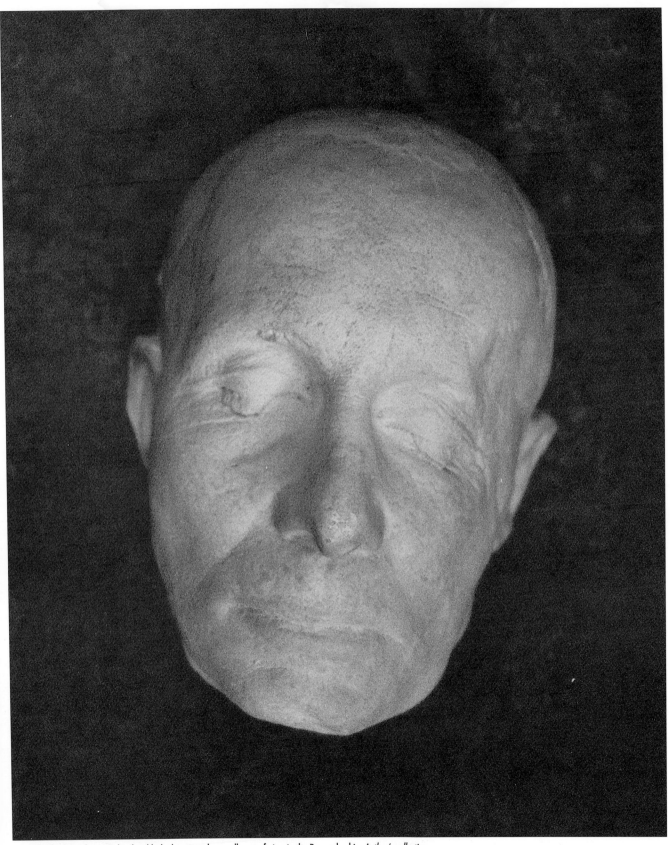

Rommel's death mask, a graphic detail locked away and normally out of view in the Rommelarchiv. *Author's collection*

Herrlingen. With Rommel were his wife and son, and his long-time aide, Captain Hermann Aldinger, Rommel's aide in the African campaign. After introducing the two visitors cordially to Manfred and Aldinger, Rommel took the generals into a downstairs room and closed the door.

In the terror that was the Reich of 1944, the visit could have meant anything: Possibly appointment to command of divisions on the Russian front or, the actual purpose, that Rommel was suspected of treason. During a conversation that lasted only a few minutes, he was given the choice of trial, with no guarantee for the safety of his family, or to commit suicide.

A personage popular enough still to be on a German postcard.

After a few minutes, Rommel emerged from the room and went upstairs to his wife. The scene was described by her in Young's *Rommel the Desert Fox*: "As he entered the room," Frau Rommel said, "There was so strange and terrible an expression on his face that I exclaimed at once, 'What is the matter with you? What has happened? Are you ill?' He looked at me and replied: 'I have come to say good-bye. In a quarter of an hour I shall be dead.'"

He took Manfred aside to explain what was happening, talked momentarily with his faithful aide, Aldinger, and shook hands with the rest of his staff in the house. Then he put on his cap and walked out with the two generals to a waiting staff car. They drove past the SS guards who had been stationed just within view of the house during the previous few weeks (not as protection for Rommel, but for surveillance).

The Rommel estate lies part way up a hill. Passing under a thick umbrella of trees ablaze with the colors of fall, the car took a left turn and lurched up toward the crest of the hill, to the edge of a wood. There Rommel followed through with the option he had agreed to. In the back seat of the car, he drank cyanide from the small flask offered him. Besides Burgdorf and Maisel, the only other witness was the driver, SS Master Sergeant Heinrich Doose. He is quoted in Irving's *The Trail of the Fox*: "I saw Rommel sitting in the back, obviously dying. He was unconscious, slumped down and sobbing—not a death rattle or groaning, but *sobbing*. His cap had fallen off. I sat him upright and put his cap back on again."

They drove directly to the adjacent, larger city of Ulm, where the community hospital was located. From the hospital an official statement was released that Rommel had died of war wounds.

Four days later, Rommel was laid to rest in the peaceful and pristine churchyard of Herrlingen's St. Andreas Church, a 10-minute walk down the hill from his home. Hitler declared a day of national mourning for the great warrior. Half a year later, in May 1945, the Third Reich was no more. Rommel's beloved Germany lay in shambles and V-E Day marked the end of the war in Europe. Only the charred hulks of tanks and the thousands of graves littered across 2,000 miles of desert marked Rommel's passage in North Africa.

Today, presiding over the vast desert sands near Tobruk is a forlorn stone marker, erected by men of the Afrika Korps. It memorializes their fallen comrades and their leader, Erwin Rommel.

A brick and stone symbol marks what came and went in the North African desert. This was set in the desert sands, probably in mid-1941, just off the Via Balbia coastal road that leads to Tobruk and eastward. Ernie Pyle wrote, "The little German cemeteries were always bordered with rows of white rocks, and in some there were phrases neatly spelled out in white rocks with a border. One that I remember said, in rough translation: 'These dead gave their spirits for the glory of Greater Germany.'" *(Here Is Your War, p. 232) National Archives*

Rommel remains a romantic figure, a tragic figure, the stuff of legends. Here, he presides over his domain of the desert in his characteristic watchful pose. *National Archives*

SELECTED BIBLIOGRAPHY

Barnett, Correlli. *The Desert Generals*. New York: The Viking Press, 1961.

Barnett, Correlli. *The Battle of El Alamein: Decision in the Desert*. New York: The Macmillan Company, 1964.

Black, Wallace and Blashfield, Jean. *Desert Warfare*. New York: Crestwood House, 1992.

Blumenson, Martin. *Kasserine Pass*. Boston: Houghton Mifflin Company, 1967.

Churchill, Winston S. *The Second World War*. Boston: Houghton Mifflin Company.

The Grand Alliance, 1950.

The Hinge of Fate, 1950.

Carlson, Lewis H. *We Were Each Other's Prisoners*. New York: Basic Books, 1997.

Collier, Richard. *The War in the Desert*. Alexandria, Va.: Time-Life Books, 1977.

Doenitz, Karl. *Memoirs: Ten Years and Twenty Days*. Cleveland and New York: The World Publishing Company, 1959.

Douglas-Home, Charles. *Rommel*. New York: Wiedenfeld & Nicholson, 1974.

Dupuy, Trevor Nevitt. *Combat Leaders of World War II*. New York: Franklin Watts, Inc., 1965.

Ferrel, Robert H. *The Eisenhower Diaries*. New York: W.W. Norton & Company, 1981.

Fraser, David. *Knight's Cross*. New York: Harper Collins Publishers, 1993.

Gelb, William. *Desperate Venture: The Story of Operation Torch, the Allied Invasion of North Africa*. New York: William Morrow and Company, Inc., 1992.

Hart, B.H. Liddell. *The Rommel Papers*. New York: Harcourt, Brace and Company, 1953.

Heckstall-Smith, Anthony. *Tobruk: The Story of a Siege*. New York: W.W. Norton & Company, 1960.

Irving, David. *The Trail of the Fox*. New York: Avon, 1977.

Leckie, Robert. *Delivered from Evil*. New York: Harper Collins Publishers, 1987.

Lewin, Ronald. *Rommel as Military Commander*. New York: Van Nostrand Reinhold Company, 1969.

Lidz, Richard. *Many Kinds of Courage*. New York: G.P. Putnam's Sons, 1980.

Mellenthin, F.W. von. *Panzer Battles: A Study of the Emplacement of Armor in the Second World War*. Translated by H. Betzler. New York: Ballantine Books, 1971.

Montgomery, Field Marshal Bernard Law. *The Memoirs of Field Marshal Montgomery*. Cleveland and New York: The World Publishing Company, 1958.

Moorehead, Alan. *The March to Tunis*. New York: Harper & Row, Publishers, 1965.

Overy, Richard. *The Road to War*. New York: The Macmillan Company, 1990.

Pimlett, Dr. John. *Rommel in His Own Words*. London: Greenhill Books, 1994.

Playfair, I.S.O., et al. *The Mediterranean and Middle East*:

Vol. 2, *The Germans Come to the Help of Their Ally (1941)*. London: Her Majesty's Stationery Office, 1956.

Vol. 3, *British Fortunes Reach Their Lowest Ebb*. London: Her Majesty's Stationery Office, 1960.

Vol. 4, *The Destruction of the Axis Forces in Africa*. London: Her Majesty's Stationery Office, 1966.

Pyle, Ernie. *Here Is Your War*. New York: Henry Holt and Company, 1943.

Rommel, Erwin. *Infantry Attacks*. London: Greenhill Books, 1990.

Sears, Stephen W. *Desert War in North Africa*. New York: American Heritage Publishing, 1967.

Speer, Albert. *Inside the Third Reich*. New York: The Macmillan Company, 1970.

Steinhoff, Johannes and Pechel, Peter and Showalter, Dennis. *Voices from the Third Reich, an Oral History*. Washington, D.C.: Regnery Gateway, 1989.

Straubing, Harold Elk. *A Taste of War*. New York: Sterling Publishing Co., Inc., 1992.

Vining, Donald. *American Diaries of World War II*. New York: Pepys Press, 1982.

Young, Desmond. *Rommel: The Desert Fox*. New York: William Morrow and Company, Inc., 1950.

INDEX